Totto-chan

The Little Girl at the Window

Totto-chan

The Little Girl at the Window

Tetsuko Kuroyanagi

Translated by
Dorothy Britton

KODANSHA INTERNATIONAL
Tokyo • New York • London

ACKNOWLEDGMENT

The three poems on page 106 and the Issa poem on page 107 are reprinted from *The Autumn Wind* by Lewis Mackenzie, 1957, courtesy of John Murray (Publishers) Ltd.

Some of the illustrations first appeared as follows:
That on the title page was for *Tonari ni kita ko* (Shikō Sha), 1976; those on pages 49, 80, 95 were covers of the journal *Kodomo no shiawase* (Sōdo Bunka), September 1970, July 1967, and 1968 and 1969; p. 9, journal *Charm Salon 10* (Senshu Kai) April 1971; pp. 32, 60, 138 were posters for Higeta Shōyu Co. 1960-70; p. 114 was in *Watashi ga chiisakatta toki ni*, (Dōshin Sha), 1967; p. 144 was for *Akaitori meisakushū* (not used).

All the original drawings are exhibited at:
  Iwasaki Chihiro Museum of Picture Books
  7-2, Shimo-shakuji 4-chome, Nerima-ku, Tokyo 177-0042.

Illustrations: Chihiro Iwasaki

Originally published in 1981, in Japanese, under the title Madogiwa no Totto-chan by Kodansha Publishers Ltd., Tokyo.

Distributed in the United States by Kodansha America, Inc., and in the United Kingdom and continental Europe by Kodansha Europe Ltd.

Published by Kodansha International Ltd., 17-14 Otowa 1-chome, Bunkyo-ku, Tokyo 112-8652, and Kodansha America, Inc.

LCC 82-80735
ISBN-13: 978-4-7700-2067-3
ISBN-10: 4-7700-2067-8

First edition, 1982
First paperback edition, 1996
10 09 08 07 06 05 04   20 19 18 17 16 15 14 13 12 11

www.kodansha-intl.com

To the memory
of
Sosaku Kobayashi

CONTENTS

🌷 The Railroad Station

They got off the Oimachi train at Jiyugaoka Station, and Mother took Totto-chan by the hand to lead her through the ticket gate. She had hardly ever been on a train before and was reluctant to give up the precious ticket she was clutching.

"May I keep it?" Totto-chan asked the ticket collector.

"No, you can't," he replied, taking it from her.

She pointed to his box filled with tickets. "Are those all yours?"

"No, they belong to the railroad station," he replied, as he snatched away tickets from people going out.

"Oh." Totto-chan gazed longingly into the box and went on, "When I grow up I'm going to sell railroad tickets!"

9

The ticket collector glanced at her for the first time. "My little boy wants a job in the station, too, so you can work together."

Totto-chan stepped to one side and took a good look at the ticket collector. He was plump and wore glasses and seemed rather kind.

"Hmm." She put her hands on her hips and carefully considered the idea. "I wouldn't mind at all working with your son," she said. "I'll think it over. But I'm rather busy just now as I'm on my way to a new school."

She ran to where Mother waited, shouting, "I'm going to be a ticket seller!"

Mother wasn't surprised, but she said, "I thought you were going to be a spy."

As Totto-chan began walking along holding Mother's hand, she remembered that until the day before she had been quite sure she wanted to be a spy. But what fun it would be to be in charge of a box full of tickets!

"That's it!" A splendid idea occurred to her. She looked up at Mother and informed her of it at the top of her voice, "Couldn't I be a ticket seller who's really a spy?"

Mother didn't reply. Under her felt hat with its little flowers, her lovely face was serious. The fact was Mother was very worried. What if they wouldn't have Totto-chan at the new school? She looked at Totto-chan skipping along the road chattering to herself. Totto-chan didn't know Mother was worried, so when their eyes met, she said gaily, "I've changed my mind. I think I'll join one of those little bands of street musicians who go about advertising new stores!"

There was a touch of despair in Mother's voice as she said, "Come on, we'll be late. We mustn't keep the headmaster waiting. No more chatter. Look where you're going and walk properly."

Ahead of them, in the distance, the gate of a small school was gradually coming into view.

🌷 The Little Girl at the Window

The reason Mother was worried was because although Totto-chan had only just started school, she had already been expelled. Fancy being expelled from the first grade!

It had happened only a week ago. Mother had been sent for by Totto-chan's homeroom teacher, who came straight to the point. "Your daughter disrupts my whole class. I must ask you to take her to another school." The pretty young teacher sighed. "I'm really at the end of my tether."

Mother was completely taken aback. What on earth did Totto-chan do to disrupt the whole class, she wondered?

Blinking nervously and touching her hair, cut in a short pageboy style, the teacher started to explain. "Well, to begin with, she opens and shuts her desk hundreds of times. I've said that no one is to open or shut their desk unless they have to take something out or put something away. So your daughter is constantly taking something out and putting something away—taking out or putting away her notebook, her pencil box, her textbooks, and everything else in her desk. For instance, say we are going to write the alphabet, your daughter opens her desk, takes out her notebook, and bangs the top down. Then she

11

opens her desk again, puts her head inside, gets out a pencil, quickly shuts the desk, and writes an 'A.' If she's written it badly or made a mistake she opens the desk again, gets out an eraser, shuts the desk, erases the letter, then opens and shuts the desk again to put away the eraser—all at top speed. When she's written the 'A' over again, she puts every single item back into the desk, one by one. She puts away the pencil, shuts the desk, then opens it again to put away the notebook. Then, when she gets to the next letter, she goes through it all again—first the note-book, then the pencil, then the eraser—opening and shutting her desk every single time. It makes my head spin. And I can't scold her because she opens and shuts it each time for a reason."

The teacher's long eyelashes fluttered even more as if she were reliving the scene in her mind.

It suddenly dawned on Mother why Totto-chan opened and shut her desk so often. She remembered how excited Totto-chan had been when she came home from her first day at school. She had said, "School's wonderful! My desk at home has drawers you pull out, but the one at school has a top you lift up. It's like a box, and you can keep all sorts of things inside. It's super!"

Mother pictured her delightedly opening and shut-ting the lid of this new desk. And Mother didn't think it was all that naughty either. Anyway, Totto-chan would probably stop doing it as soon as the novelty wore off. But all she said to the teacher was, "I'll speak to her about it."

The teacher's voice rose in pitch as she continued, "I wouldn't mind if that was all."

Mother flinched as the teacher leaned forward.

"When she's not making a clatter with her desk, she's standing up. All through class!"

"Standing up? Where?" asked Mother, surprised.

"At the window," the teacher replied crossly.

"Why does she stand at the window?" Mother asked, puzzled.

"So she can invite the street musicians over!" she almost shrieked.

The gist of the teacher's story was that after an hour of almost constantly banging her desk top, Totto-chan would leave her desk and stand by the window, looking out. Then, just as the teacher was beginning to think that as long as she was quiet she might just as well stay there, Totto-chan would suddenly call out to a passing band of garishly dressed street musicians. To Totto-chan's delight and the teacher's tribulation, the classroom was on the ground floor looking out on the street. There was only a low hedge in between, so anyone in the classroom could easily talk to people going by. When Totto-chan called to them, the street musicians would come right over to the window. Whereupon, said the teacher, Totto-chan would announce the fact to the whole room, "Here they are!" and all the children would crowd by the window and call out to the musicians.

"Play something," Totto-chan would say, and the little band, which usually passed the school quietly, would put on a rousing performance for the pupils with their clarinet, gongs, drums, and samisen, while the poor teacher could do little but wait patiently for the din to stop.

Finally, when the music finished, the musicians would leave and the students would go back to their seats. All except Totto-chan. When the teacher asked, "Why are you still at the window?" Totto-chan replied, quite seriously, "Another band might come by. And, anyway, it would be such a shame if the others came back and we missed them."

"You can see how disruptive all this is, can't you?" said the teacher emotionally. Mother was beginning to sympathize with her when she began again in an even shriller voice, "And then, besides . . . "

"What else does she do?" asked Mother, with a sinking feeling.

"What else?" exclaimed the teacher. "If I could even count the things she does I wouldn't be asking you to take her away."

The teacher composed herself a little, and looked straight at Mother. "Yesterday, Totto-chan was standing at the window as usual, and I went on with the lesson thinking she was just waiting for the street musicians, when she suddenly called out to somebody, 'What are you doing?' From where I was I couldn't see who she was talking to, and I wondered what was going on. Then she called out again, 'What are you doing?' She wasn't addressing anyone in the road but somebody high up somewhere. I couldn't help being curious, and tried to hear the reply, but there wasn't any. In spite of that, your daughter kept on calling out, 'What are you doing?' so often I couldn't teach, so I went over to the window to see who your daughter was talking to. When I put my head out of the window and looked up, I saw it was a pair of swallows making a nest under the classroom eaves. She was talking to the swallows! Now, I understand children, and so I'm not saying that talking to swallows is nonsense. It is just that I feel it is quite unnecessary to ask swallows what they are doing in the middle of class."

Before Mother could open her mouth to apologize, the teacher went on, "Then there was the drawing class episode. I asked the children to draw the Japanese flag, and all the others drew it correctly but your daughter started drawing the navy flag—you know, the one with the rays. Nothing wrong with that, I thought. But then she suddenly started to draw a fringe all around it. A fringe! You know, like those fringes on youth group banners. She's probably seen one somewhere. But before I realized what she was doing, she had drawn a yellow fringe that went right

off the edge of the paper and onto her desk. You see, her flag took up most of the paper, so there wasn't enough room for the fringe. She took her yellow crayon and all around her flag she made hundreds of strokes that extended beyond the paper, so that when she lifted up the paper her desk was a mass of dreadful yellow marks that wouldn't come off no matter how hard we rubbed. Fortunately, the lines were only on three sides."

Puzzled, Mother asked quickly, "What do you mean, only three sides?"

Although she seemed to be getting tired, the teacher was kind enough to explain. "She drew a flagpole on the left, so the fringe was only on three sides of the flag."

Mother felt somewhat relieved. "I see, only on three sides."

Whereupon the teacher said very slowly, emphasizing each word, "But most of the flagpole went off the paper, too, and is still on the desk as well."

Then the teacher got up and said coldly, as a sort of parting shot, "I'm not the only one who is upset. The teacher in the classroom next door has also had trouble."

Mother obviously had to do something about it. It wasn't fair to the other pupils. She'd have to find another school, a school where they would understand her little girl and teach her how to get along with other people.

The school they were on their way to was one Mother had found after a good deal of searching.

Mother did not tell Totto-chan she had been expelled. She realized Totto-chan wouldn't understand what she had done wrong and she didn't want her to

16

get any complexes, so she decided not to tell Totto-chan until she was grown-up. All Mother said was, "How would you like to go to a new school? I've heard of a very nice one."

"All right," said Totto-chan, after thinking it over. "But . . . "

"What is it now?" thought Mother. "Does she realize she's been expelled?"

But a moment later Totto-chan was asking joyfully, "Do you think the street musicians will come to the new school?"

The New School

When she saw the gate of the new school, Totto-chan stopped. The gate of the school she used to go to had fine concrete pillars with the name of the school in large characters. But the gate of this new school simply consisted of two rather short posts that still had twigs and leaves on them.

"This gate's growing," said Totto-chan. "It'll probably go on growing till it's taller than the telephone poles!"

The two "gateposts" were clearly trees with roots. When she got closer, she had to put her head to one side to read the name of the school because the wind had blown the sign askew.

"To-mo-e Ga-ku-en."

Totto-chan was about to ask Mother what "Tomoe" meant, when she caught a glimpse of something that made her think she must be dreaming. She squatted down and peered through the shrubbery to get a better look, and she couldn't believe her eyes.

17

"Mother, is that really a train? There, in the school grounds!"

For its classrooms, the school had made use of six abandoned railroad cars. To Totto-chan it seemed something you might dream about. A school in a train!

The windows of the railroad cars sparkled in the morning sunlight. But the eyes of the rosy-cheeked little girl gazing at them through the shrubbery sparkled even more.

🌷 "I Like This School!"

A moment later, Totto-chan let out a whoop of joy and started running toward the "train school," calling out to Mother over her shoulder, "Come on, hurry, let's get on this train that's standing still."

Startled, Mother began to run after her. Mother had been on a basketball team once, so she was faster than Totto-chan and caught hold of her dress just as she reached a door.

"You can't go in yet," said Mother, holding her back. "The cars are classrooms, and you haven't even been accepted here yet. If you really want to get on this train, you'll have to be nice and polite to the headmaster. We're going to call on him now, and if all goes well, you'll be able to go to this school. Do you understand?"

Totto-chan was awfully disappointed not to get on the "train" right away, but she decided she had better do as Mother told her.

"All right," she said. And then added, "I like this school a lot."

Mother felt like telling her it wasn't a matter of

whether she liked the school but of whether the headmaster liked her. But she just let go of Totto-chan's dress, took hold of her hand, and started walking toward the headmaster's office.

All the railroad cars were quiet, for the first classes of the day had begun. Instead of a wall, the not very spacious school grounds were surrounded by trees, and there were flower beds full of red and yellow flowers.

The headmaster's office wasn't in a railroad car, but was on the right-hand side of a one-story building that stood at the top of a semicircular flight of about seven stone steps opposite the gate.

Totto-chan let go of Mother's hand and raced up the steps, then turned around abruptly, almost causing Mother to run into her.

"What's the matter?" Mother asked, fearing Totto-chan might have changed her mind about the school.

Standing above her on the top step, Totto-chan whispered to Mother in all seriousness, "The man we're going to see must be a stationmaster!"

Mother had plenty of patience as well as a great sense of fun. She put her face close to Totto-chan's and whispered, "Why?"

Totto-chan whispered back, "You said he was the headmaster, but if he owns all these trains, he must be a stationmaster."

Mother had to admit it was unusual for a school to make use of old railroad cars, but there was no time to explain. She simply said, "Why don't you ask him yourself? And, anyway, what about Daddy? He plays the violin and owns several violins, but that doesn't make our house a violin shop, does it?"

"No, it doesn't," Totto-chan agreed, catching hold of Mother's hand.

🌷 The Headmaster

When Mother and Totto-chan went in, the man in the office got up from his chair.

His hair was thin on top and he had a few teeth missing, but his face was a healthy color. Although he wasn't very tall, he had solid shoulders and arms and was neatly dressed in a rather shabby black three-piece suit.

With a hasty bow, Totto-chan asked him spiritedly, "What are you, a schoolmaster or a stationmaster?"

Mother was embarrassed, but before she had time to explain, he laughed and replied, "I'm the headmaster of this school."

Totto-chan was delighted. "Oh, I'm so glad," she said, "because I want to ask you a favor. I'd like to come to your school."

The headmaster offered her a chair and turned to Mother. "You may go home now. I want to talk to Totto-chan."

Totto-chan had a moment's uneasiness, but somehow felt she would get along all right with this man.

"Well, then, I'll leave her with you," Mother said bravely, and shut the door behind her as she went out.

The headmaster drew over a chair and put it facing Totto-chan, and when they were both sitting down close together, he said, "Now then, tell me all about yourself. Tell me anything at all you want to talk about."

"Anything I like?" Totto-chan had expected him to ask questions she would have to answer. When he said she could talk about anything she wanted, she was so happy she began straight away. It was all a bit higgledy-piggledy, but she talked for all she was worth. She told the headmaster how fast the train went that they had come on; how she had asked the ticket collector but he wouldn't let her keep her ticket; how pretty her homeroom teacher was at the other school; about the swallows' nest; about their brown dog, Rocky, who could do all sorts of tricks; how she used to go snip-snip with the scissors inside her mouth at kindergarten and the teacher said she mustn't do that because she might cut her tongue off, but she did it anyway; how she always blew her nose because Mother scolded her if it was runny; what a good swimmer Daddy was, and how he could dive as well. She went on and on. The headmaster would laugh, nod, and say, "And then?" And Totto-chan was so happy she kept right on talking. But finally she ran out of things to say. She sat with her mouth closed trying hard to think of something.

"Haven't you anything more you can tell me?" asked the headmaster.

What a shame to stop now, Totto-chan thought. It was such a wonderful chance. Wasn't there anything else she could talk about, she wondered, racking her brains? Then she had an idea.

She could tell him about the dress she was wearing that day. Mother made most of her dresses, but this one came from a shop. Her clothes were always torn when she came home in the late afternoon. Some of the rips were quite bad. Mother never knew how they got that way. Even her white cotton panties

21

were sometimes in shreds. She explained to the headmaster that they got torn when she crossed other people's gardens by crawling under their fences, and when she burrowed under the barbed wire around vacant lots. So this morning, she said, when she was getting dressed to come here, all the nice dresses Mother had made were torn so she had to wear one Mother had bought. It had small dark red and gray checks and was made of jersey, and it wasn't bad, but Mother thought the red flowers embroidered on the collar were in bad taste. "Mother doesn't like the collar," said Totto-chan, holding it up for the headmaster to see.

After that, she could think of nothing more to say no matter how hard she tried. It made her rather sad. But just then the headmaster got up, placed his large, warm hand on her head, and said, "Well, now you're a pupil of this school."

Those were his very words. And at that moment Totto-chan felt she had met someone she really liked for the very first time in her life. You see, up till then, no one had ever listened to her for so long. And all that time the headmaster hadn't yawned once or looked bored, but seemed just as interested in what she had to say as she was.

Totto-chan hadn't learned how to tell time yet, but it did seem like a rather long time. If she had been able to, she would have been astonished, and even more grateful to the headmaster. For, you see, Mother and Totto-chan arrived at the school at eight, and when she had finished talking and the headmaster had told her she was a pupil of the school, he looked at his pocket watch and said, "Ah, it's time for lunch." So the headmaster must have

22

listened to Totto-chan for four solid hours!

Neither before nor since did any grown-up listen to Totto-chan for as long as that. And, besides, it would have amazed Mother and her homeroom teacher to think that a seven-year-old child could find enough to talk about for four hours nonstop.

Totto-chan had no idea then, of course, that she had been expelled and that people were at their wit's end to know what to do. Having a naturally sunny disposition and being a bit absent-minded gave her an air of innocence. But deep down she felt she was considered different from other children and slightly strange. The headmaster, however, made her feel safe and warm and happy. She wanted to stay with him forever.

That's how Totto-chan felt about Headmaster Sosaku Kobayashi that first day. And, luckily, the headmaster felt the same about her.

Lunchtime

The headmaster took Totto-chan to see where the children had lunch. "We don't have lunch in the train," he explained, "but in the Assembly Hall." The Assembly Hall was at the top of the stone steps Totto-chan had come up earlier. When they got there, they found the children noisily moving desks and chairs about, arranging them in a circle. As they stood in one corner and watched, Totto-chan tugged at the headmaster's jacket and asked, "Where are the rest of the children?"

"This is all there are," he replied.

"All there are?" Totto-chan couldn't believe it.

There were as many children as this in just one grade at the other school.

"You mean there are only about fifty children in the whole school?"

"That's all," said the headmaster.

Everything about this school was different from the other one, thought Totto-chan.

When everyone was seated, the headmaster asked the pupils if they had all brought something from the ocean and something from the hills.

"Yes!" they chorused, opening their various lunchboxes.

"Let's see what you've got," said the headmaster, strolling about in the circle of desks and looking into each box while the children squealed with delight.

"How funny," thought Totto-chan. "I wonder what he means by 'something from the ocean and something from the hills.'" This school was different. It was fun. She never thought lunch at school could be as much fun as this. The thought that tomorrow she would be sitting at one of those desks, showing the headmaster her lunch with "something from the ocean and something from the hills" made Totto-chan so happy she wanted to jump for joy.

As he inspected the lunchboxes, the headmaster's shoulders were bathed in the soft noontime light.

Totto-chan Starts School

After the headmaster had said, "Now you're a pupil of this school," Totto-chan could hardly wait for the next day to dawn. She had never looked forward to a day so much. Mother usually had trouble getting

Totto-chan out of bed in the morning, but that day she was up before anyone else, all dressed and waiting with her schoolbag strapped to her back.

The most punctual member of the household —Rocky, the German shepherd—viewed Totto-chan's unusual behavior with suspicion, but after a good stretch, he positioned himself close to her, expecting something to happen.

Mother had a lot to do. She busily made up a box lunch containing "something from the ocean and something from the hills" while she gave Totto-chan her breakfast. Mother also put Totto-chan's train pass in a plastic case and hung it around Totto-chan's neck on a cord so she wouldn't lose it.

"Be a good girl," said Daddy, his hair all tousled.

"Of course." Totto-chan put on her shoes and opened the front door, then turned around, bowed politely, and said, "Goodbye, everybody."

Tears welled up in Mother's eyes as she watched Totto-chan go out. It was hard to believe that this vivacious little girl, setting off so obediently and happily, had just been expelled from school. She prayed fervently that all would go well this time.

A moment later Mother was startled to see Totto-chan remove the train pass and hang it around Rocky's neck instead. "Oh dear . . . " thought Mother, but she decided to say nothing but wait and see what happened.

After Totto-chan put the cord with the pass around Rocky's neck, she squatted down and said to him, "You see? This pass doesn't fit you at all."

The cord was much too long and the pass dragged on the ground.

"Do you understand? This is my pass, not yours.

You won't be able to get on the train. I'll ask the headmaster, though, and the man at the station, and see if they'll let you come to school, too.

Rocky listened attentively at first, ears pointed, but after giving the pass a few licks, he yawned. Totto-chan went on, "The classroom train doesn't move, so I don't think you'll need a ticket to get on that one, but today you'll just have to stay home and wait for me."

Rocky always used to walk with Totto-chan as far as the gate of the other school and then come back home. Naturally, he was expecting to do the same today.

Totto-chan took the cord with the pass off Rocky's neck and carefully hung it around her own. She called out once more to Mother and Daddy, "Goodbye!"

Then she ran off, without a backward glance, her bag flapping against her back. Rocky bounded along happily beside her.

The way to the station was almost the same as to the old school, so Totto-chan passed dogs and cats she knew, as well as children from her former class.

Should she show them her pass and impress them, Totto-chan wondered? But she didn't want to be late, so she decided not to that day, and hurried on.

When Totto-chan turned right at the station instead of left as usual, poor Rocky stopped and looked around anxiously. Totto-chan was already at the ticket gate, but she went back to Rocky, who stood, looking mystified.

"I'm not going to the other school any more. I'm going to a new one now."

Totto-chan put her face against Rocky's. His ears

were smelly, as usual, but to Totto-chan it was a nice smell.

"Bye-bye," she said and, showing the man her pass, she started climbing up the steep station stairs. Rocky whimpered softly and watched until Totto-chan was out of sight.

The Classroom in the Train

No one had arrived yet when Totto-chan got to the door of the railroad car the headmaster had told her would be her classroom. It was an old-fashioned car, one that still had a door handle on the outside. You took hold of the handle with both hands and slid the door to the right. Totto-chan's heart was beating fast with excitement as she peeped inside.

"Ooh!"

Studying here would be like going on a perpetual journey. The windows still had baggage racks above them. The only difference was that there was a blackboard at the front of the car, and the lengthwise seats had been replaced by school desks and chairs all facing forward. The hand straps had gone, too, but everything else had been left just as it was. Totto-chan went in and sat down at someone's desk. The wooden chairs resembled those at the other school, but they were so much more comfortable she could sit on them all day. Totto-chan was so happy and liked the school so much, she made a firm decision to come to school every day and never take any holidays.

Totto-chan looked out of the window. She knew the train was stationary, but—was it because the flowers and trees in the school grounds were swaying

27

slightly in the breeze?—it seemed to be moving.

"I'm so happy!" she finally said out loud. Then she pressed her face against the window and made up a song just as she always did whenever she was happy.

I'm so happy,
So happy am I!
Why am I happy?
Because . . .

Just at that moment someone got on. It was a girl. She took her notebook and pencil box out of her schoolbag and put them on her desk. Then she stood on tiptoe and put the bag on the rack. She put her shoe bag up there, too. Totto-chan stopped singing and quickly did the same. After that a boy got on. He stood at the door and threw his bag on the baggage rack as if he were playing basketball. It bounced off and fell on the floor. "Bad shot!" said the boy, taking aim again from the same place. This time it stayed on. "Nice shot!" he shouted, followed by "No, bad shot," as he scrambled onto the desk and opened his bag to get out his notebook and pencil box. His failure to do this first evidently made it count as a miss.

Eventually there were nine pupils in the car. They comprised the first grade at Tomoe Gakuen.

They would all be traveling together on the same train.

Lessons at Tomoe

Going to school in a railroad car seemed unusual enough, but the seating arrangements turned out to be unusual, too. At the other school each pupil was assigned a specific desk. But here they were allowed to sit anywhere they liked at any time.

After a lot of thought and a good look around, Totto-chan decided to sit next to the girl who had come after her that morning because the girl was wearing a pinafore with a long-eared rabbit on it.

The most unusual thing of all about this school, however, was the lessons themselves.

Schools normally schedule one subject, for example, Japanese, the first period, when you just do Japanese; then, say, arithmetic the second period, when you just do arithmetic. But here it was quite different. At the beginning of the first period, the teacher made a list of all the problems and questions in the subjects to be studied that day. Then she would say, "Now, start with any of these you like."

So whether you started on Japanese or arithmetic or something else didn't matter at all. Someone who liked composition might be writing something, while behind you someone who liked physics might be boiling something in a flask over an alcohol burner, so that a small explosion was liable to occur in any of the classrooms.

This method of teaching enabled the teachers to observe—as the children progressed to higher grades —what they were interested in as well as their way of thinking and their character. It was an ideal way for teachers to really get to know their pupils.

As for the pupils, they loved being able to start with their favorite subject, and the fact that they had all day to cope with the subjects they disliked meant they could usually manage them somehow. So study was mostly independent, with pupils free to go and consult the teacher whenever necessary. The teacher would come to them, too, if they wanted, and explain any problem until it was thoroughly understood. Then pupils would be given further exercises to work at alone. It was study in the truest sense of the word, and it meant there were no pupils just sitting inattentively while the teacher talked and explained.

The first grade pupils hadn't quite reached the stage of independent study, but even they were allowed to start with any subject they wanted.

Some copied letters of the alphabet, some drew pictures, some read books, and some even did calisthenics. The girl next to Totto-chan already knew all her alphabet and was writing it into her notebook. It was all so unfamiliar that Totto-chan was a bit nervous and unsure what to do.

Just then the boy sitting behind her got up and walked toward the blackboard with his notebook, apparently to consult the teacher. She sat at a desk beside the blackboard and was explaining something to another pupil. Totto-chan stopped looking around the room and, with her chin cupped in her hands, fixed her eyes on his back as he walked. The boy dragged his leg, and his whole body swayed dreadfully. Totto-chan wondered at first if he was doing it on purpose, but she soon realized the boy couldn't help it.

Totto-chan went on watching him as the boy came back to his desk. Their eyes met. The boy smiled. Totto-chan hurriedly smiled back. When he sat down at the desk behind her—it took him longer than other children to sit down—she turned around and asked, "Why do you walk like that?"

30

He replied quietly, with a gentle voice that sounded intelligent, "I had polio."

"Polio?" Totto-chan repeated, never having heard the word before.

"Yes, polio," he whispered. "It's not only my leg, but my hand, too." He held it out. Totto-chan looked at his left hand. His long fingers were bent and looked as if they were stuck together.

"Can't they do anything about it?" she asked, concerned. He didn't reply, and Totto-chan became embarrassed, wishing she hadn't asked. But the boy said brightly, "My name's Yasuaki Yamamoto. What's yours?"

She was so glad to hear him speak in such a cheerful voice that she replied loudly, "I'm Totto-chan."

That's how Yasuaki Yamamoto and Totto-chan became friends.

The sun made it quite hot inside the train. Someone opened a window. The fresh spring breeze blew through the car and tossed the children's hair about with carefree abandon.

In this way Totto-chan's first day at Tomoe began.

Sea Food and Land Food

Now it was time for "something from the ocean and something from the hills," the lunch hour Totto-chan had looked forward to so eagerly.

The headmaster had adopted the phrase to describe a balanced meal—the kind of food he expected you to bring for lunch in addition to your rice. Instead of the usual "Train your children to eat everything," and "Please see that they bring a nutritiously balanced lunch," this headmaster asked

31

parents to include in their children's lunchboxes "something from the ocean and something from the hills."

"Something from the ocean" meant sea food—things such as fish and *tsukuda-ni* (tiny crustaceans and the like boiled in soy sauce and sweet saké), while "something from the hills" meant food from the land—like vegetables, beef, pork, and chicken.

Mother was very impressed by this and thought that few headmasters were capable of expressing such an important rule so simply. Oddly enough, just having to choose from two categories made preparing lunch seem simpler. And besides, the

headmaster pointed out that one did not have to think too hard or be extravagant to fulfill the two requirements. The land food could be just *kinpira gobō* (spicy burdock) or an omelette, and the sea food merely flakes of dried bonito. Or simpler still, you could have *nori* (a kind of seaweed) for "ocean" and a pickled plum for "hills."

Just as the day before, when Totto-chan had watched so enviously, the headmaster came and looked in all the lunchboxes.

"Have you something from the ocean and something from the hills?" he asked, checking each one. It was so exciting to discover what each had brought from the ocean and from the hills.

Sometimes a mother had been too busy and her child had only something from the hills, or only something from the ocean. But never mind. As the headmaster made his round of inspection, his wife followed him, wearing a cook's white apron and holding a pan in each hand. If the headmaster stopped in front of a pupil saying, "Ocean," she would dole out a couple of boiled *chikuwa* (fish rolls) from the "Ocean" saucepan, and if the headmaster said, "Hills," out would come some chunks of soy-simmered potato from the "Hills" saucepan.

No one would have dreamed of saying, "I don't like fish rolls," any more than thinking what a fine lunch so-and-so has or what a miserable lunch poor so-and-so always brings. The children's only concern was whether they had satisfied the two requirements—the ocean and the hills—and if so their joy was complete and they were all in good spirits.

Beginning to understand what "something from the ocean and something from the hills" was all about, Totto-chan had doubts whether the lunch her mother had so hastily prepared that morning would be approved. But when she opened the lunchbox, she found such a marvelous lunch inside, it was all she could do to stop herself shouting, "Oh, goody, goody!"

Totto-chan's lunch contained bright yellow scrambled eggs, green peas, brown *denbu*, and pink flaked cod roe. It was as colorful as a flower garden.

"How very pretty," said the headmaster.

Totto-chan was thrilled. "Mother's a very good cook," she said.

"She is, is she?" said the headmaster. Then he pointed to the *denbu*. "All right. What's this? Is it from the ocean or the hills?"

Totto-chan looked at it, wondering which was right. It was the color of earth, so maybe it was from the hills. But she couldn't be sure.

"I don't know," she said.

The headmaster then addressed the whole school, "Where does *denbu* come from, the ocean or the hills?"

After a pause, while they thought about it, some shouted, "Hills," and others shouted, "Ocean," but no one seemed to know for certain.

"All right. I'll tell you," said the headmaster. "*Denbu* is from the ocean."

"Why?" asked a fat boy.

Standing in the middle of the circle of desks, the headmaster explained, "*Denbu* is made by scraping the flesh of cooked fish off the bones, lightly roasting and crushing it into fine pieces, which are then dried and flavored."

"Oh!" said the children, impressed. Then someone

34

asked if they could see Totto-chan's *denbu.*

"Certainly," said the headmaster, and the whole school trooped over to look at Totto-chan's *denbu.* There must have been children who knew what *denbu* was but whose interest had been aroused, as well as those who wanted to see if Totto-chan's *denbu* was any different from the kind they had at home. So many children sniffed at Totto-chan's *denbu* that she was afraid the bits might get blown away.

Totto-chan was a little nervous that first day at lunch, but it was fun. It was fascinating wondering what was sea food and what was land food, and she learned that *denbu* was made of fish, and Mother had remembered to include something from the ocean and something from the hills, so all in all everything had been all right, she thought contentedly.

And the next thing that made Totto-chan happy was that when she started to eat the lunch Mother had made, it was delicious.

❦ *"Chew It Well!"*

Normally one starts a meal by saying, "*Itadakimasu*" (I gratefully partake), but another thing that was different at Tomoe Gakuen was that first of all everybody sang a song. The headmaster was a musician and he had made up a special "Song to Sing before Lunch." Actually, he just made up the words and set them to the tune of the well-known round "Row, Row, Row Your Boat." The words the headmaster made up went like this:

> Chew, chew, chew it well,

Everything you eat;
　Chew it and chew it and chew it and chew it,
　Your rice and fish and meat!

It wasn't until they had finished singing this song that the children all said "*Itadakimasu.*"

The words fitted the tune of "Row, Row, Row Your Boat" so well that even years later many of the pupils firmly believed it had always been a song you sang before eating.

The headmaster may have made up the song because he had lost some of his teeth, but he was always telling the children to eat slowly and take plenty of time over meals while enjoying pleasant conversation, so it is more likely he made up this song to remind them of that.

After they had sung the song at the tops of their voices, the children all said "*Itadakimasu*" and settled down to "something from the ocean and something from the hills."

For a while the Assembly Hall was quiet.

❧ School Walks

After lunch Totto-chan played in the school grounds with the others before returning to the classroom, where the teacher was waiting for them.

"You all worked hard this morning," she said, "so what would you like to do this afternoon?"

Before Totto-chan could even begin to think about what she wanted to do, there was a unanimous shout.

"A walk!"

"All right," said the teacher, and the children all

began rushing to the doors and dashing out. Totto-chan used to go for walks with Daddy and Rocky, but she had never heard of a school walk and was astounded. She loved walks, however, so she could hardly wait.

As she was to find out later, if they worked hard in the morning and completed all the tasks the teacher had listed on the blackboard, they were generally allowed to go for a walk in the afternoon. It was the same whether you were in the first grade or the sixth grade.

Out of the gate they went—all nine first grade pupils with their teacher in their midst and began walking along the edge of a stream. Both banks of the stream were lined with large cherry trees that had only recently been in full bloom. Fields of yellow mustard flowers stretched as far as the eye could see. The stream has long since disappeared, and apartment buildings and stores now crowd the area. But in those days Jiyugaoka was mostly fields.

"We go as far as Kuhonbutsu Temple," said the girl with the rabbit on her pinafore dress. Her name was Sakko-chan.

"We saw a snake by the pond there last time," said Sakko-chan. "There's an old well in the temple grounds which they say a shooting star fell into once."

The children chatted away about anything they liked as they walked along. The sky was blue and the air was filled with the fluttering of butterflies.

After they had walked for about ten minutes, the teacher stopped. She pointed to some yellow flowers, and said, "Look at these mustard flowers. Do you know why flowers bloom?"

She explained about pistils and stamens while the children crouched by the road and examined the flowers. The teacher told them how butterflies helped flowers bloom. And, indeed, the butterflies seemed very busy helping.

Then the teacher set off again, so the children stopped inspecting the flowers and stood up. Someone said, "They don't look like pistols, do they?"

Totto-chan didn't think so either, but like the other children, she was sure that pistils and stamens were very important.

After they had walked for about another ten minutes, a thickly wooded park came into view. It surrounded the temple called Kuhonbutsu. As they entered the grounds the children scattered in various directions.

"Want to see the shooting-star well?" asked Sakko-chan, and naturally Totto-chan agreed and ran after her.

The well looked as if it was made of stone and came up to their chests. It had a wooden lid. They lifted the lid and peered in. It was pitch dark, and Totto-chan could see something like a lump of concrete or stone, but nothing whatsoever resembling the twinkling star she had imagined. After staring inside for a long time, she asked, "Have you seen the star?"

Sakko-chan shook her head. "No, never."

Totto-chan wondered why it didn't shine. After thinking about it for a while, she said, "Maybe it's asleep."

Opening her big round eyes even wider, Sakko-chan asked, "Do stars sleep?"

"I think they must sleep in the daytime and then

38

wake up at night and shine," said Totto-chan quickly because she wasn't really sure.

Then the children gathered together and walked around the temple grounds. They laughed at the bare bellies of the two Deva Kings that stood on either side of the gate, guarding the temple, and gazed with awe at the statue of Buddha in the semi-darkness of the Main Hall. They placed their feet in the great footprint in a stone said to have been made by a Tengu—a long-nosed goblin. They strolled around the pond, calling out "Hello!" to the people in rowboats. And they played hopscotch to their hearts' content with the glossy black pebbles around the graves. Everything was new to Totto-chan, and she greeted each discovery with an excited shout.

"Time to go back!" said the teacher, as the sun began to dip, and the children set off for the school along the road between the mustard blossoms and the cherry trees.

Little did the children realize then that these walks—a time of freedom and play for them—were in reality precious lessons in science, history, and biology.

Totto-chan had already made friends with all the children and felt she had known them all her life.

"Let's go for a walk again tomorrow!" she shouted to them all on the way back.

"Yes, let's!" they shouted back, hopping and skipping.

The butterflies were still going busily about their business, and the song of birds filled the air. Totto-chan's heart was bursting with joy.

Each day at Tomoe Gakuen was filled with surprises for Totto-chan. So eager was she to go to school that mornings never dawned soon enough. And when she got home she couldn't stop talking—telling Rocky and Mother and Daddy all about what she had done at school that day and what fun it had been, and all the surprises. Mother would finally have to say, "That's enough, dear. Stop talking and have your afternoon snack."

Even when Totto-chan was quite accustomed to the new school, she still had mountains of things to talk about every day. And Mother rejoiced to think that this was so.

One day, on her way to school in the train, Totto-chan suddenly began wondering whether Tomoe had a school song. Wanting to find out as soon as possible, she could hardly wait to get there. Although there were still two more stations to go, she went and stood by the door, ready to jump out as soon as the train pulled into Jiyugaoka. A lady getting on at the station before saw the little girl at the door and naturally thought she was getting off. When the child remained motionless—poised like a runner, all set and "on your marks"—the lady muttered, "I wonder what's the matter with her."

When the train arrived at the station, Totto-chan was off it in a flash. By the time the young conductor was calling out, "Jiyugaoka! Jiyugaoka!"—one foot smartly on the platform before the train had come to a proper halt—Totto-chan had already disappeared through the exit.

The moment she was inside the railroad-car classroom, Totto-chan asked Taiji Yamanouchi, who was already there, "Tai-chan, does this school have a song?"

Tai-chan, who liked physics, replied after some thought, "I don't think it has."

"Oh," said Totto-chan, pensively. "Well, I think it ought to. We had a lovely one at my other school."

She began singing it at the top of her voice:

> Tho' shallow the waters of Senzoku Pond,
> Deep is our learning of vistas beyond . . .

Totto-chan had only gone to the school a short time, and the words were difficult, but she had no trouble remembering the song. That part, at any rate.

Tai-chan seemed impressed. By this time other pupils had arrived, and they, too, seemed impressed by the big words she used.

"Let's get the headmaster to make up a school song!" said Totto-chan.

"Yes, let's!" agreed the others, and they all trooped over to the headmaster's office.

After listening to Totto-chan sing the song from the other school and after considering the children's request, the headmaster said, "All right, I'll have a school song for you by tomorrow morning."

"Promise you will!" chorused the children, and they filed out to return to their classroom.

Next morning, there was a notice in each classroom requiring everyone to assemble in the school grounds. Totto-chan joined the others, all agog. Bringing a blackboard out into the center of the grounds, the headmaster said, "Now then, here's a song for Tomoe, your school." He drew five parallel lines on the blackboard and wrote out the following notes:

Then he raised both his arms like a conductor, saying, "Now let's try and sing it, all together!"

While the headmaster beat time and led the singing, the whole school, all fifty students, joined in:

To-mo-e, To-mo-e, To—mo—e!

"Is that all there is?" asked Totto-chan, after a brief pause.

"Yes, that's all," said the headmaster, proudly.

"Something with fancy words would have been nicer," said Totto-chan in a terribly disappointed voice. "Something like 'Tho' shallow the waters of Senzoku Pond.' "

"Don't you like it?" asked the headmaster, flushed but smiling. "I thought it was rather good."

Nobody liked it. It was far too simple. They'd rather have no song at all, it appeared, then anything as simple as that.

The headmaster seemed rather sorry, but he wasn't angry, and proceeded to wipe it off the blackboard. Totto-chan felt that they had been rather rude, but after all she had something a bit more impressive in mind.

The truth was that nothing could have expressed the headmaster's love for the children and the school more, but the children weren't old enough to

42

realize that. They soon forgot about wanting a school song, and the headmaster probably never considered one necessary in the first place. So when the tune had been rubbed off the blackboard, that was the end of the matter, and Tomoe Gakuen never did have a school song.

🌷 *"Put It All Back!"*

Totto-chan had never labored so hard in her life. What a day that was when she dropped her favorite purse down the toilet! It had no money in it, but Totto-chan loved the purse so much she even took it to the toilet with her. It was a truly beautiful purse made of red, yellow, and green checked taffeta. It was square and flat, with a silver Scotch terrier rather like a brooch over the triangular flap of the fastening.

Now Totto-chan had a curious habit. Ever since she was small, whenever she went to the toilet, she made it a point to peer down the hole after she had finished. Consequently, even before she started going to elementary school, she had already lost several hats, including a straw one and a white lace one. Toilets, in those days, had no flush systems, only a sort of cesspool underneath, so the hats were usually left floating there. Mother was always telling Totto-chan not to peer down the hole after she had finished using the toilet.

That day, when Totto-chan went to the toilet before school started, she forgot Mother's warning, and before she knew it, she found herself peering down the hole. She must have loosened her hold on the purse at that moment, for it slipped out of her hand and dropped down the hole with a splash. Totto-chan let out a cry as it disappeared into the darkness below.

But Totto-chan refused to shed tears or give up the purse as lost. She went to the janitor's shed and got a large, long-handled wooden ladle used for watering the garden. The handle was almost twice as long as she was, but that did not deter her in the least. She went around with it to the back of the school and tried to find the opening through which the cesspool was emptied. She imagined it would be on the out-side wall of the toilet, but after searching in vain she finally noticed a round concrete manhole cover about a yard away. Lifting it off with difficulty, she discovered an opening that was undoubtedly the one she was looking for. She put her head inside.

"Why, it's as big as the pond at Kuhonbutsu!" she exclaimed.

Then she began her task. She started ladling out the contents of the cesspool. At first she tried the area in which she had dropped the purse. But the tank was deep and dark and quite extensive, since it served three separate toilets. Moreover, she was in danger of falling in herself if she put her head in too far, so she decided to just keep on ladling and hope for the best, emptying her ladle onto the ground around the hole.

She inspected each ladleful, of course, to see if it contained the purse. She hadn't thought it would take her long to find, but there was no sign of the purse. Where could it be? The bell rang for the beginning of class.

What should she do, she wondered, but having

gone so far she decided to continue. She ladled with renewed vigor.

There was quite a pile on the ground when the headmaster happened to pass by.

"What are you doing?" he asked Totto-chan.

"I dropped my purse," she replied, as she went on ladling, not wanting to waste a moment.

"I see," said the headmaster, and walked away, his hands clasped behind his back as was his habit when he went for a stroll.

Time went by and she still hadn't found the purse. The foul-smelling pile was getting higher and higher.

The headmaster came by again. "Have you found it?" he inquired.

"No," replied Totto-chan, from the center of the pile, sweating profusely, her cheeks flushed.

The headmaster came closer and said in a friendly tone, "You'll put it all back when you've finished, won't you?" Then he went off again, as he had done before.

"Yes," Totto-chan replied cheerfully, as she went on with her work. Suddenly a thought struck her. She looked at the pile. "When I've finished I can put all the solid stuff back, but what do I do about the water?"

The liquid portion was disappearing fast into the earth. Totto-chan stopped working and tried to figure out how she could get that part back into the tank, too, since she had promised the headmaster to put it all back. She finally decided the thing to do was to put in some of the wet earth.

The pile was a real mountain by now and the tank was almost empty, but there was still no sign of the purse. Maybe it had stuck to the rim of the tank or to the bottom. But Totto-chan didn't care. She was satisfied she had done all she could. Totto-chan's satisfaction was undoubtedly due in part to the self-respect the headmaster made her feel by not scolding her and by trusting her. But that was too complicated for Totto-chan to realize then.

Most adults, on discovering Totto-chan in such a situation, would have reacted by exclaiming, "What on earth are you doing!" or "Stop that, it's dangerous!" or, alternatively, offering to help.

Imagine just saying, "You'll put it all back when you've finished, won't you?" What a marvelous headmaster, thought Mother when she heard the story from Totto-chan.

After the incident, Totto-chan never peered down the hole any more after using the toilet. And she felt the headmaster was someone she could trust completely, and she liked him more than ever.

Totto-chan kept her promise and put everything back into the tank. It was a terrible job getting it out, but putting it back was much quicker. She put some of the wet earth in, too. Then she smoothed the ground, put the cover back properly, and took the ladle back to the janitor's shed.

That night before she went to bed Totto-chan thought about the beautiful purse she had dropped into the darkness. She was sad about losing it, but the day's exertion had made her so tired it was not long before she was fast asleep.

Meanwhile, at the scene of her toil, the damp earth shimmered in the moonlight like some beautiful thing.

And somewhere the purse rested quietly.

🌷 Totto-chan's Name

Totto-chan's real name was Tetsuko. Before she was born all Mother's and Daddy's friends and relatives said they were sure the baby would be a boy. It was their first child, and they believed it. So they decided to name the baby Toru. When the baby turned out to be a girl, they were a bit disappointed, but they both liked the Chinese character for *tōru* 徹 (which means to penetrate, to carry far, to be clear and resonant, as a voice) so they made it into a girl's name by using its Chinese-derived pronunciation *tetsu* and adding the suffix *ko* often used for girls' names.

So everybody called her Tetsuko-chan (*chan* is the familiar form of the *san* used after a person's name). But it didn't sound quite like Tetsuko-chan to her. Whenever anyone asked her what her name was, she would answer, "Totto-chan." She even thought that *chan* was part of her name, too.

Daddy sometimes called her Totsky, as if she were a boy. He'd say, "Totsky! Come and help me take these bugs off the roses!" But except for Daddy and Rocky everybody else called her Totto-chan, and although she wrote her name as Tetsuko in her notebooks at school, she still went on thinking of herself as Totto-chan.

🌷 Radio Comedians

Yesterday Totto-chan was very upset. Mother had said, "You mustn't listen to any more comedians on the radio."

When Totto-chan was a little girl, radios were large and made of wood. They were very elegant.

47

Theirs was rectangular with a rounded top, and a big speaker in front covered with pink silk and carved arabesques. It had two control knobs.

Even before she started school, Totto-chan liked to listen to *rakugo* comedians, pressing her ear against the pink silk. She thought their jokes were terribly funny. Mother had never objected to her listening to them until yesterday.

Last night some of Daddy's friends from the orchestra came to their house to practice string quartets in the living room.

"Mr. Tsunesada Tachibana, who plays the cello, has brought you some bananas," said Mother.

Totto-chan was thrilled. She bowed politely to Mr. Tachibana, and by way of thanks exclaimed to her mother, "Hey, Ma, this is pretty goddam good!"

After that Totto-chan had to listen in secret when Mother and Daddy were out. When the comedians were good, she would laugh uproariously. If any grown-ups had been watching, they might well have wondered how such a small girl could understand such difficult jokes. But there's no doubt that children have an innate sense of humor. No matter how young they are, they always know when something's really funny.

A Railroad Car Arrives

"There's a new railroad car coming tonight," said Miyo-chan during the lunchtime break. Miyo-chan was the headmaster's third daughter and was in Totto-chan's class.

There were already six cars lined up together as classrooms, but one more was coming. Miyo-chan

48

said it was going to be a library car. They were all terribly excited.

"I wonder what route it will take to get to the school," someone said.

It was a challenging topic. There was a momentary hush.

"Maybe it will come along the Oimachi Line tracks and then branch off this way at that level crossing," someone suggested.

"Then it would have to derail," said someone else.

"Maybe they'll just bring it on a cart," said another.

"There wouldn't be a cart big enough to hold one of those cars," someone pointed out immediately.

"I suppose not . . . "

Ideas petered out. The children realized a railroad car certainly wouldn't fit on a cart or even a truck.

"Rails!" said Totto-chan after much thought. "You know, they're probably going to lay some rails right here to the school!"

"From where?" asked someone.

"Where? From wherever the train is now," said Totto-chan, beginning to think her idea wasn't such a good one, after all. She had no idea where the car was coming from, and, anyway, they wouldn't pull down houses and things in order to lay tracks in a straight line to the school.

After much fruitless discussion of one possibility after another, the children finally decided not to go home that afternoon but to wait and see the car arrive. Miyo-chan was elected to go and ask her father, the headmaster, if they could all remain at school until that night. It was some while before she came back.

"The car is arriving terribly late tonight," she said, "after all the other trains have stopped running. Anybody who really wants to see it will have to go home first and ask permission. Then they can come back if they like with their pajamas and a blanket after they've had their dinner."

"Wow!" The children were more excited than ever.

"He said to bring our pajamas?"

"And blankets?"

That afternoon no one could concentrate on the lessons. After school, the children in Totto-chan's class went straight home, all hoping they'd be lucky enough to see each other again that night complete with pajamas and blankets.

As soon as she reached home, Totto-chan said to Mother, "A train's coming. We don't know how it's going to get there. Pajamas and a blanket. May I go?"

What mother could grasp the situation with that kind of explanation? Totto-chan's mother had no idea what she meant. But judging by the serious look on her daughter's face, she guessed something unusual was afoot.

Mother asked Totto-chan all sorts of questions. She finally discovered what it was all about and what exactly was going to happen. She thought Totto-chan ought to see it, as she wouldn't have many such opportunities. She even thought she'd like to see the car arrive herself.

Mother got out Totto-chan's pajamas and a blanket, and after dinner she took her to the school. About ten children were there. They included some of the older students who had heard of the event. A couple of other mothers, too, had come with their children. They looked as if they would like to stay, but after entrusting their children to the headmaster's care, they went home.

"I'll wake you up when it comes," the children were assured by the headmaster as they lay down in the Assembly Hall wrapped in their blankets.

The children thought they wouldn't be able to sleep for wondering how the train would get there. But after so much excitement, they were tired and

51

soon became drowsy. Before they could say, "Be sure and wake me up," most of them fell fast asleep.

"It's here! It's here!"

Awakened by a babel of voices, Totto-chan jumped up and ran through the school grounds and out the gate. A great big railroad car was just visible in the morning haze. It was like a dream—a train coming along the road without tracks making no sound. It had come on a large trailer pulled by a tractor from the Oimachi Line depot. Totto-chan and the others learned something they didn't know before —that there was something called a tractor that could pull a trailer, which was much bigger than a cart. They were impressed.

The car moved slowly along the deserted morning road mounted on the trailer.

Soon there was a great commotion. There were no giant cranes in those days, so to get the car off the trailer and to its destination in the school grounds was a tremendous operation. The men who brought it had to lay several big logs under the car and gradually roll it off the trailer onto the schoolyard.

"Watch carefully," said the headmaster, "they're called rollers. Rolling power is being used to move that big car."

The children looked on earnestly.

"Heave-ho, heave-ho," chanted the workmen as they toiled, and the sun itself seemed to be rising in time to their rhythmic cries.

Like the other six already at the school, this car, which had carried so many people, had its wheels removed. Its traveling life was over. From now on it would carry the sound of children's laughter.

As the boys and girls stood there in the morning

sunshine in their pajamas, they were so happy they couldn't contain their joy and kept jumping up and down, clasping the headmaster around the neck and swinging from his arms.

Staggering under the onslaught, the headmaster smiled happily. Seeing his joy, the children smiled, too.

And none of them ever forgot how happy they were.

The Swimming Pool

That was a red-letter day for Totto-chan. It was the first time she had ever swum in a pool. And without a stitch on!

It happened in the morning. The headmaster said to them all, "It's become quite hot all of a sudden, so I think I'll fill the pool."

"Wow!" everybody cried, jumping up and down. Totto-chan and the first grade children cried "Wow" too, and jumped up and down with even greater excitement than the older students. The pool at Tomoe was not rectangular like most pools, as one end was narrower than the other. It was shaped pretty much like a boat. The lay of the land probably had something to do with it. But nonetheless, the pool was a large and splendid one. It was situated between the classrooms and the Assembly Hall.

All during their lessons, Totto-chan and the others kept stealing glances out of the windows at the pool. When empty it had been littered with fallen leaves just like the playground. But now that it was clean and beginning to fill up, it started to look like a real swimming pool.

Lunchtime finally arrived, and when the children were all gathered around the pool, the headmaster said, "We'll do some exercises and then have a swim."

"Don't I need a swimsuit to go swimming?" thought Totto-chan. When she went to Kamakura with Mother and Daddy, she took a swimsuit, a rubber ring, and all sorts of things. She tried to remember if the teacher had asked them to bring swimsuits.

Then, just as if he had read her thoughts, the headmaster said, "Don't worry about swimsuits. Go and look in the Assembly Hall."

When Totto-chan and the other first graders got to the Assembly Hall the bigger children were taking off their clothes with shrieks of delight as if they were going to have a bath. They ran out, one after the other, stark naked, into the school grounds. Totto-chan and her friends hurriedly followed them. In the warm breeze it felt wonderful not to have any clothes on. When they got to the top of the steps outside the Assembly Hall they found the others already doing warm-up exercises. Totto-chan and her classmates ran down the steps in their bare feet.

The swimming instructor was Miyo-chan's elder brother—the headmaster's son and an expert in gymnastics. He wasn't a teacher at Tomoe but he was on the swimming team of a university. His name was the same as the school's—Tomoe. Tomoe-san wore swimming trunks.

After their exercises, the children let out screams as cold water was poured over them, and then they jumped into the pool. Totto-chan didn't go in until she had watched some of the others and satisfied

54

herself they could stand. It wasn't hot, like a bath, but it was lovely and big, and as far as you could stretch your arms there was nothing but water.

Thin children, plump children, boys, girls—they were all laughing and shouting and splashing in their birthday suits.

What fun, thought Totto-chan, and what a lovely feeling! She was only sorry Rocky couldn't come to school. She was sure that if he knew he could go in without a swimsuit he'd be in the pool, too.

You might wonder why the headmaster allowed the children to swim naked. There were no rules about it. If you brought your suit and wanted to wear it, that was perfectly all right. On the other hand, like today, when you suddenly decided to go in and hadn't a suit, that was perfectly all right, too. And why did he let them swim in the nude? Because he thought it wasn't right for boys and girls to be morbidly curious about the differences in their bodies, and he thought it was unnatural for people to take such pains to hide their bodies from each other.

He wanted to teach the children that all bodies are beautiful. Among the pupils at Tomoe were some who had had polio, like Yasuaki-chan, or were very small, or otherwise handicapped, and he felt if they bared their bodies and played together it would rid them of feelings of shame and help to prevent them developing an inferiority complex. As it turned out, while the handicapped children were shy at first, they soon began to enjoy themselves, and finally they got over their shyness completely.

Some parents were worried about the idea and provided their offspring with swimsuits which they insisted should always be worn. Little did they know how seldom the suits were used. Observing children like Totto-chan—who right from the start decided swimming naked was best—and those who said they had forgotten to bring their suits and went in anyway, most of them became convinced it was much more fun swimming naked like the others, so all they did was make sure they took wet swimsuits home! Consequently, almost all the children at Tomoe became as brown as berries all over, and there were hardly any with white swimsuit marks.

❦ The Report Card

Looking neither right nor left, her bag flapping against her back, Totto-chan ran all the way home from the station. Anyone seeing her would have thought something terrible had happened. She had started running as soon as she was out of the school gate.

Once home, she opened the front door and called out, "I'm back!" and went to look for Rocky. He was lying on the porch, cooling off, with his belly flat against the floor. Totto-chan didn't say a word. She sat down in front of Rocky, took her bag off her back, and took out a report card. It was her very first report card. She opened it so Rocky could clearly see her marks.

"Look!" she said proudly. There were A's and B's and other characters. Naturally, Totto-chan didn't know yet whether A was better than B or whether B was better than A, so it would have been even harder for Rocky to know. But Totto-chan wanted to show her very first report card to Rocky before anyone else, and she was sure Rocky would be delighted.

When Rocky saw the paper in front of his face, he sniffed it, then gazed up at Totto-chan.

"You're impressed, aren't you?" said Totto-chan. "But it's full of difficult words so you probably can't read all of it."

Rocky tilted his head as if he was having another good look at the card. Then he licked Totto-chan's hand.

"Good," she said with satisfaction, getting up. "Now I'll go and show it to Mother."

After Totto-chan had gone, Rocky got up and found himself a cooler spot. Then he let himself down again slowly, and closed his eyes. It wasn't only Totto-chan who would have said that the way his eyes were closed it really seemed as if he was thinking about that report card.

🌷 Summer Vacation Begins

"We are going camping tomorrow. Please come to the school in the evening with blankets and pajamas," said the note from the headmaster that Totto-chan took home and showed to Mother. Summer vacation began the following day.

"What does camping mean?" asked Totto-chan.

Mother was wondering, too, but she replied, "Doesn't it mean you're probably going to put up tents somewhere outdoors and sleep in them? Sleeping in a tent you can see the moon and the stars. I wonder where they'll set up the tents. There's no mention of fares so it's probably somewhere near the school."

That night, after Totto-chan had gone to bed, she couldn't get to sleep for ages. The idea of going camping sounded rather scary—a tremendous adventure—and her heart beat very fast.

The following morning she started packing as soon as she woke up. But that evening, as her blanket was placed on top of the knapsack that held her pajamas and she said goodbye and set off, she felt very small and frightened.

When the children were gathered at the school, the headmaster said, "Now then, all of you, come to the Assembly Hall." When they got there he went up onto the small stage carrying something stiff and starchy. It was a green tent.

"I'm going to show you how to pitch a tent," he said, spreading it out. "Please watch carefully."

All alone, puffing and blowing, he pulled ropes this way and set up poles that way, and before you could say "Jack Robinson," there stood a beautiful tent!

"Come on, then," he said. "Now you're going to set up tents all over the Assembly Hall and start camping."

Mother imagined, as anyone would have, that they would put up the tents outdoors, but the headmaster had other ideas. In the Assembly Hall the children would be all right even if it rained in the night or got a bit cold.

With delighted shouts of "We're camping, we're camping!" the children divided into groups, and, with the help of the teachers, they finally managed to set up the required number of tents. One tent could sleep about three children. Totto-chan quickly got into her pajamas, and soon children were happily crawling in and out of this tent and that one. There was much visiting to and fro.

When everyone was in pajamas, the headmaster sat down in the middle where they could all see him and talked to them about his travels abroad.

Some of the children lay in their tents with just their heads showing, while others sat up properly, and some lay with their heads on older children's laps, all listening to his tales of foreign countries they had never seen and sometimes never even heard of. The headmaster's stories were fascinating, and at times they felt as if the children described in lands across the sea were friends.

And so it happened that this simple event—sleeping in tents in the Assembly Hall—became for the children a happy and valuable experience they would never forget. The headmaster certainly knew how to make children happy.

When the headmaster finished speaking and the light in the Assembly Hall had been turned out, all the children went into their own tents. Laughter could be heard from some; whispers from others; while from a tent at the far end came the sound of a scuffle. Gradually silence fell.

It was camping without any moon or stars, but the children enjoyed it thoroughly. To them that little Assembly Hall seemed like a real camping ground, and memory wrapped that night in moonbeams and starlight forever.

♨ The Great Adventure

Two days after they camped in the Assembly Hall, the day of Totto-chan's great adventure finally came to pass. It was the day of her appointment with Yasuaki-chan. And it was a secret that neither Mother nor Daddy nor Yasuaki-chan's parents knew. She had invited Yasuaki-chan to her tree.

The students at Tomoe each had a tree in the school grounds they considered their own climbing tree. Totto-chan's tree was at the edge of the grounds near the fence beside the lane leading to Kuhonbutsu. It was a large tree and slippery to climb, but if you climbed it skillfully you could get to a fork about six feet from the ground. The fork was as comfortable as a hammock. Totto-chan used to go there dur-

ing recess and after school and sit and look off into the distance or up at the sky, or watch the people going by below.

The children considered "their" trees their own private property, so if you wanted to climb someone else's tree you had to ask their permission very politely, saying, "Excuse me, may I come in?"

Because Yasuaki-chan had had polio he had never climbed a tree, and couldn't claim one as his own. That's why Totto-chan decided to invite him to her tree. They kept it a secret because they thought people were sure to make a fuss if they knew.

When she left home, Totto-chan told her mother she was going to visit Yasuaki-chan at his home in Denenchofu. She was telling a lie, so she tried not to look at Mother but kept her eyes on her shoelaces. But Rocky followed her to the station, so when they parted company, she told him the truth.

"I'm going to let Yasuaki-chan climb my tree!" she said.

When Totto-chan reached the school, her train pass flapping around her neck, she found Yasuaki-chan waiting by the flower beds in the grounds that were deserted now that it was summer vacation. He was only a year older than Totto-chan, but he always sounded much older when he spoke.

When Yasuaki-chan saw Totto-chan, he hurried toward her, dragging his leg and holding his arms out in front to steady himself. Totto-chan was thrilled to think they were going to do something secret, and she giggled. Yasuaki-chan giggled, too.

Totto-chan led Yasuaki-chan to her tree, and then, just as she had thought it out the night before, she ran to the janitor's shed and got a ladder, which she dragged over to the tree and leaned against the trunk so that it reached the fork. She climbed up quickly and, holding the top of the ladder, called down, "All right, try climbing up!"

Yasuaki-chan's arms and legs were so weak it seemed he could not even get on the first rung without help. So Totto-chan hurried down the ladder backward and tried pushing Yasuaki-chan up from behind. But Totto-chan was so small and slender that it was all she could do to hold onto Yasuaki-chan, let alone keep the ladder steady. Yasuaki-chan took his foot off the bottom rung and stood beside the ladder, his head bowed. Totto-chan realized for the first time that it was going to be more difficult than she had thought. What should she do?

She wanted so badly to have Yasuaki-chan climb her tree, and he had been looking forward to it so much. She went around and faced him. He looked so disconsolate that she puffed out her cheeks and made a funny face to cheer him up.

"Wait! I've got an idea!"

She ran back to the janitor's shed and pulled out one thing after another to see if she could find something that would help. She finally discovered a stepladder. It would remain steady so she wouldn't have to hold it.

She dragged the stepladder over, amazed at her own strength, and was delighted to find that it almost reached the fork.

"Now, don't be afraid," she said in a big-sisterly voice. "This isn't going to wobble."

Yasuaki-chan looked nervously at the stepladder. Then he looked at Totto-chan, drenched in perspiration. Yasuaki-chan was sweating profusely, too. He looked up at the tree. Then, with determination, he placed a foot on the first rung.

Neither of them was conscious of the time it took Yasuaki-chan to reach the top of the stepladder. The hot summer sun beat down, but they had no thoughts for anything except getting Yasuaki-chan to the top of the stepladder. Totto-chan got underneath him and lifted his feet up while steadying his bottom with her head. Yasuaki-chan struggled with all his might, and finally reached the top.

"Hooray!"

But from there it was hopeless. Totto-chan jumped onto the fork, but no matter how she tried, she couldn't get Yasuaki-chan onto the tree from the stepladder. Clutching the stepladder Yasuaki-chan looked at Totto-chan. She suddenly felt like crying. She had wanted so badly to invite Yasuaki-chan onto her tree and show him all sorts of things.

But she didn't cry. She was afraid that if she did, Yasuaki-chan might start crying, too.

Instead she took hold of his hand, with its fingers all stuck together because of the polio. It was bigger than hers and his fingers were longer. She held his hand for a long time. Then she said, "Lie down and I'll try and pull you over."

If any grown-ups had seen her standing on the fork of the tree starting to pull Yasuaki-chan—who was lying on his stomach on the stepladder—onto the tree, they would have let out a scream. It must have looked terribly precarious.

But Yasuaki-chan trusted Totto-chan completely. And Totto-chan was risking her life for him. With her tiny hands clutching his, she pulled with all her might. From time to time a large cloud would mercifully protect them from the blistering sun.

At long last, the two stood face to face on the tree. Brushing her damp hair back, Totto-chan bowed politely and said, "Welcome to my tree."

Yasuaki-chan leaned against the trunk smiling rather bashfully. He said, "May I come in?"

Yasuaki-chan was able to see vistas he had never glimpsed before. "So this is what it's like to climb a tree," he said happily.

They stayed on the tree for a long time and talked about all sorts of things.

"My sister in America says they've got something there called television," said Yasuaki-chan with enthusiasm. "She says that when it comes to Japan we'll be able to sit at home and watch sumo wrestling. She says it's like a box."

Totto-chan didn't understand yet how much it would mean to Yasuaki-chan, who couldn't go very far afield, to be able to watch all sorts of things at home.

She simply wondered how sumo wrestlers could get inside a box in your own house. Sumo wrestlers were so big! But it was fascinating all the same. In those days nobody knew about television. Yasuaki-chan was the first to tell Totto-chan about it.

The cicadas were singing and the two children were so happy. And for Yasuaki-chan it was the first and last time he ever climbed a tree.

The Bravery Test

"What's scary, smells bad, and tastes good?"
They liked this riddle so much that even though

they knew the answer, Totto-chan and her friends never tired of saying to one another, "Ask me the riddle about what's scary and smells bad!"

The answer was, "A demon in the toilet eating a bean-jam bun!"

The way the Tomoe Bravery Test ended would have made a good riddle too. "What's scary, itches, and makes you laugh?"

The night they set up tents in the Assembly Hall and went camping, the headmaster announced, "We're going to hold a Bravery Test one night at Kuhonbutsu Temple. Hands up if you want to be a ghost."

About seven boys vied for the privilege. When the children assembled at the school on the appointed evening, the boys who were going to be ghosts brought costumes they had made themselves and went off to hide in the temple grounds.

"We'll scare you to death!" they said as they left.

The remaining thirty or so children divided themselves into small groups of about five and set off for Kuhonbutsu at staggered intervals. They were supposed to walk right around the temple grounds and the graveyard and then come back to the school.

The headmaster explained that although this was a test to see how brave they were, it would be perfectly all right if anybody wanted to come back without finishing the course.

Totto-chan had brought a flashlight she had borrowed from Mother.

"Don't lose it," Mother had said.

Some of the boys said they were going to catch the ghosts and brought butterfly nets, while others brought string saying they were going to tie them up.

It was dark by the time the headmaster had explained what they were to do, and groups had been formed by playing "stone, paper, scissors." Squealing with excitement, the first group set off out of the school gate. Finally it was time for Totto-chan's group to go.

The headmaster said no ghosts would appear before they got to Kuhonbutsu Temple, but the children weren't too sure about that and proceeded nervously until they reached the entrance to the temple, from where they could see the guardian Deva Kings. The temple grounds seemed pitch dark in spite of the moon being out. It was pleasant and spacious there by day, but now, not knowing when they would encounter one of the ghosts, the children were so terrified they could hardly bear it. "Eee!" someone would scream as a tree rustled in the breeze, or "Here's a ghost!" as someone's leg touched something soft. In the end it seemed as if even the friend whose hand one was holding might be a ghost. Totto-chan made up her mind not to go all the way to the graveyard. That's where the ghosts were bound to be waiting, and anyway she felt she now knew all about bravery tests and could go back. The others in her group made the same decision at the same time—it was reassuring not to be the only one—and they all ran back as fast as their legs could carry them.

When they got to the school they found the groups that had left before them already there. It seemed that almost everybody had been too scared to go as far as the graveyard.

Just then, a boy with a white cloth over his head came through the gate crying, accompanied by a teacher. He was one of the ghosts and had been crouching in the graveyard the whole time, but nobody had come and he got more and more scared and finally went outside and was found crying in the road by the patrolling teacher who brought him back. While they were all trying to cheer the boy up, a second ghost came back crying with another boy who was also crying. The one who was the ghost had also been hiding in the graveyard and when he heard someone running toward it, he leaped out to try and scare him and they collided head-on. Hurt, and frightened to death, the two of them came running back together. It was so funny, and with the great relief that came after being so scared, the

children laughed their heads off. The ghosts laughed and cried at the same time. Soon one of Totto-chan's classmates, whose surname was Migita, arrived back. He was wearing a ghost's hood made of newspaper and he was furious because nobody had come into the graveyard.

"I've been waiting there all this time," he complained, scratching the mosquito bites on his arms and legs.

"A ghost's been bitten by mosquitoes," someone said, and everyone began laughing again.

"Well, I'd better go and bring back the rest of the ghosts," said Mr. Maruyama, the fifth grade home-room teacher, setting off. He rounded up ghosts he found standing bewildered under street lights, and ghosts who had been so frightened they had gone home. He brought them all back to the school.

After that night Tomoe students weren't frightened of ghosts any more. For, after all, even ghosts themselves get frightened, don't they?

🌷 The Rehearsal Hall

Totto-chan walked sedately. Rocky walked sedately, too, looking up at Totto-chan from time to time. That could only mean one thing: they were on their way to peek in at Daddy's rehearsal hall. Normally, Totto-chan would be running as fast as she could, or walking this way and that looking for something she had dropped, or going across other people's gardens, one after the other, ducking under their fences.

Daddy's rehearsal hall was about a five-minute walk from their house. He was the concertmaster of an orchestra, and being a concertmaster meant he played the violin. Once when she was taken to a concert, what had intrigued Totto-chan was that after the people had all finished clapping, the perspiring conductor turned toward the audience, got down from his podium, and shook hands with Daddy who had been playing the violin. Then Daddy stood up, and all the rest of the orchestra stood up, too.

"Why did they shake hands?" Totto-chan had whispered.

"The conductor wants to thank the orchestra for having played so well, so he shook hands with Daddy as the representative of the orchestra as a way of saying thank you," explained Mother.

The reason Totto-chan liked going to the rehearsal hall was that, unlike school, where there were mostly children, here they were all grown-ups, and they played all sorts of instruments. Besides, the conductor, Mr. Rosenstock, spoke such funny Japanese.

Josef Rosenstock, Daddy had told her, was a very famous conductor in Europe, but a man called Hitler was starting to do terrible things there, so Mr. Rosenstock had to escape and come all the way to Japan in order to continue to make music. Daddy said he greatly admired Mr. Rosenstock. Totto-chan didn't understand the world situation, but just at that time Hitler had started persecuting Jews. If it hadn't been for that, Rosenstock would never have come to Japan, and the orchestra that composer Kosçak Yamada had founded would probably never have made such progress in the short time it did, through the efforts of this conductor of international standing. Rosenstock demanded of the orchestra the same level of performance he would have expected from a first-class orchestra in Europe. That's why Rosenstock always wept at the end of rehearsals.

"I try so hard and you don't respond."

Hideo Saito, the cellist, who used to conduct while Rosenstock was resting, spoke the best German and would reply for them all, "We are doing the best we can. Our technique is still not good enough. I assure you our failure is not deliberate."

The intricacies of the situation escaped her, but sometimes Mr. Rosenstock would get so red in the face it seemed as if steam should be coming out of his head, and he began shouting in German. At times like that, Totto-chan would retire from her favorite window where she had been watching—chin in hands—and would crouch on the ground with Rocky, hardly daring to breathe, and wait for the music to begin again.

But normally Mr. Rosenstock was very nice and his Japanese was quite amusing.

"Very good, Kuroyanagi-san," he would say with a funny accent when they had played well. Or, "Wonderful!"

Totto-chan had never been inside the rehearsal hall. She liked to peek in at the window and listen to the music. So when they stopped for a break and the musicians came outside to have a smoke, Daddy often found her there.

"Oh, there you are, Totsky!" he would say.

If Mr. Rosenstock spotted her he'd say, "Good morning" or "Good day" in his funny accent, and although she was big now, he would pick her up as he did when she was little and put his cheek against hers. It embarrassed her a bit, but she liked Mr. Rosenstock. He wore glasses with thin silver rims and had a large nose and was not very tall. But he had a fine handsome face that you could immediately recognize as an artist's.

Totto-chan liked the rehearsal hall. It was rather Western in style, and a bit dilapidated.

The wind that blew from Senzoku Pond carried the sound of the music far beyond the rehearsal hall. Sometimes the call of the goldfish (*kingyo*) vendor would blend with the music:

Kin - gyo,   ee   Kin - gyo!

🌷 A Trip to a Hot Spring

Summer vacation came to an end, and the day of the trip to the hot spring resort finally arrived. It was considered by the students to be Tomoe's main event. Not many things surprised Mother, but when Totto-chan came home from school one day and asked, "May I go on the hot spring trip with the others?" she was flabbergasted. She had heard of old people visiting hot springs in groups but not first graders. But after she read the headmaster's letter carefully, she thought it was an excellent idea and was filled with admiration for his plan. The trip was to be a "Seaside School" at a place called Toi on the Izu Peninsula in Shizuoka. There was a hot spring right in the sea, where the children could both swim and take hot baths. The trip would last three days and two nights. The father of one of the Tomoe students had a vacation home there, where all fifty of the Tomoe students from first through sixth grades could stay. Mother, of course, agreed.

The Tomoe students assembled at the school on the appointed day before setting off.

"Now then," said the headmaster when they were all together. "We're traveling by train and by ship, and I don't want any of you to get lost. Do you understand? All right, off we go!"

That was the only instruction he gave, yet when they got on the Toyoko train at Jiyugaoka, the children were amazingly well behaved. Nobody ran up and down the cars, and the only talking was done quietly among those sitting next to each other. The Tomoe pupils had never once been told they should get in line and walk properly and keep quiet on the train and not drop litter on the floor when they ate their food. Their daily school life had somehow instilled into them that they mustn't push people smaller or weaker than themselves; that unruly behavior was something to be ashamed of; that whenever they came across litter they should pick it up; and that they should try not to do anything that annoyed or disturbed others. Strangest of all was that Totto-chan, who only a few months before had been upsetting her whole school by talking to street musicians out of the window in the middle of class, stayed at her desk and did her lessons properly from the very day she started at Tomoe. If any of the teachers from the other school could have seen her now, sitting properly with the others in the train, they would have said, "It must be someone else!"

At Numazu they embarked on a ship that was just like what they had all dreamed about. It wasn't a big ship, but they were all so excited that they inspected every corner of the deck, feeling this or hanging from that. When it finally sailed, the children waved to the townsfolk on the pier. They hadn't gone far before it started to rain, however, and they had to go inside. Soon the sea became very rough. Totto-chan began to feel ill, as did some others. But just then, one of the older boys got up and stood amidships, pretending to be a stabilizer. When the ship rolled he would run to one side, saying "Oops!" Then he would run the other way with another "Oops!" It was so funny the children couldn't help laughing even though they felt so seasick, and they were still laughing when the ship arrived at Toi. The curious thing was that after they disembarked, the poor "Oops" boy began to feel sick just when everyone else had recovered and was feeling fine!

Toi Spa was in a quiet, beautiful village on the sea surrounded by wooded hills. After a short rest the teachers took the children down to the sea. It wasn't like the swimming pool at school so they wore their swimsuits.

The hot spring in the sea was most unusual. It was not enclosed so there was no line to set off the hot spring from the rest of the sea. If you crouched down where you were told was the hot spring, the hot water came up to your neck and it felt lovely, just like being in a hot bath. If you wanted to go into the sea from the hot spring, all you had to do was move about fifteen feet sideways, and the water gradually got cooler. The further you went, the colder it got, and you knew you were in the sea. So, after you had been swimming about in the sea and began to feel cold, all you had to do was to hurry back to the hot spring and have a hot bath right up to your neck! It was like being at home. And it looked so funny. While the bathing-capped children were swimming about normally in the regular sea, the ones in the hot spring part were relaxing in a circle chatting just as if they were in a bath. Anyone watching would have thought, "Why even youngsters act just like old people when they get in a hot spring bath."

In those days the seashore was so deserted it was like being on their own private beach, and the children enjoyed this unusual hot spring sea-bathing to the utmost. When they got back to the house in the evening after staying in the water so long, their fingers were a mass of wrinkles.

Each night, once they were tucked into their quilts, the children took turns telling ghost stories. Totto-chan and the other first graders got so frightened they cried. But in spite of their tears, they would ask, "And then what happened?"

Unlike camping inside the school and the Bravery Test, the three-day stay at Toi Spa was a real-life experience. For example, they were sent in turns to buy vegetables and fish for dinner, and when strangers asked them what school they went to and where they were from, they had to answer politely. Some of the children nearly got lost in the woods. Others swam so far they couldn't get back and had everyone worried. Others cut their feet on broken glass on the beach. In each case everyone had to do their best to help.

But mostly it was all fun. There was a forest full of cicadas and a shop where you could buy popsicles. And they met a man on the beach who was building a big wooden boat all by himself. It was already boat-shaped, and the first thing each morning they ran down to the beach to see how much more he had done. The man gave Totto-chan a very long and curly wood shaving.

"How about a souvenir photograph?" asked the headmaster on the day they were to leave. They had never had a photograph taken of them all together and the children were excited at the idea. But no sooner was the teacher ready with her camera than someone had gone to the toilet; then someone else had his gym shoes on the wrong feet and had to change them around. When the teacher finally said, "Is everyone ready?" one or two of the children were lying on the ground, having become tired of holding their poses so long. The whole process took a very long time.

But that photograph, with the sea in the background and each child posing according to his or her fancy, became a treasured possession of each of them. One look at it and memories would flood back —the boat trip, the hot spring, the ghost stories, and the "Oops" boy. Totto-chan never forgot that first happy summer vacation.

Those were the days when you could still find crayfish in the pond near their house in Tokyo, and the garbageman's cart was pulled by a great big ox.

🌷 Eurythmics

After summer vacation was over, the second semester began, for in Japan the school year starts in April. In addition to the children in her own class, Totto-chan had made friends with all the older boys and girls, thanks to the various gatherings during summer vacation. And she grew to like Tomoe Gakuen even more.

Besides the fact that classes at Tomoe were different from those at ordinary schools, a great deal more time was devoted to music. There were all sorts of music lessons, which included a daily period of eurythmics—a special kind of rhythmic education devised by a Swiss music teacher and composer, Emile Jaques-Dalcroze. His studies first became known about 1904. His system was rapidly adopted all over Europe and America and training and research institutes sprang up everywhere. Here is the story of how Dalcroze's eurythmics came to be adopted at Tomoe.

Before starting Tomoe Gakuen, the headmaster, Sosaku Kobayashi, went to Europe to see how children were being educated abroad. He visited a great many elementary schools and talked to educators. In Paris, he met Dalcroze, a fine composer as well as an educator.

Dalcroze had spent a long time wondering how children could be taught to hear and feel music in their minds rather than just with their ears; how to make them feel music as a thing of movement rather than a dull, lifeless subject; how to awaken a child's sensitivity.

Eventually, after watching the way children jumped and skipped and romped about, he hit on the idea of creating rhythmic exercises, which he called eurythmics.

Kobayashi attended the Dalcroze school in Paris for over a year and learned this system thoroughly. Many Japanese have been influenced by Dalcroze —the composer Kosçak Yamada; the originator of modern dance in Japan, Baku Ishii; the Kabuki actor Ichikawa Sadanji II; the modern drama pioneer Kaoru Osannai; the dancer Michio Ito. All of these people felt that Dalcroze's teachings were fundamental to many of the arts. But Sosaku Kobayashi was the first to apply it to elementary education in Japan.

If you asked him what eurythmics was, he would reply, "It's a sport that refines the body's mechanism; a sport that teaches the mind how to use and control the body; a sport that enables the body and mind to understand rhythm. Practicing eurythmics makes the personality rhythmical. And a rhythmical personality is beautiful and strong, conforming to and obeying the laws of nature."

Totto-chan's classes began with training the body to understand rhythm. The headmaster would play the piano on the small stage in the Assembly Hall and the children, wherever they stood, would start walking in time to the music. They could walk in whatever manner they liked, except that it wasn't good to bump into others, so they tended to go in the same circular direction. If they thought the music was in two-beat time, they would wave their arms up and down, like a conductor, as they walked. As for their feet, they were not supposed to tramp heavily, but that didn't mean they were to walk with toes pointed either, as in ballet. They were told to walk completely relaxed, as if they were dragging their toes. The most important thing was naturalness, so they could walk in any way they felt was right. If the rhythm changed to three-beat time, they waved their arms accordingly and adjusted their pace to the tempo, walking faster or slower as required. They had to learn to raise and lower their arms to fit rhythms up to six-beat time. Four-beat time was simple enough:

"Down, around you, out to the sides, and up."

But when it came to five beats it was:

"Down, around you, out in front, out to the sides, and up."

While for six beats, the arms went:

"Down, around you, out in front, around you again, out to the sides, and up."

So when the beat kept changing it was pretty difficult.

What was even harder was when the headmaster would call out:

"Even if I change my tempo on the piano don't you change until I tell you to!"

Suppose they were walking in two-beat time and the music changed to three beats, the children had to keep on walking in duple time while hearing the triple rhythm. It was very hard, but the headmaster said it was to cultivate the children's powers of concentration.

Finally he would shout, "You can change now!"

With relief, the children would immediately change to the triple rhythm. But that was when they had to be especially alert. In the time it took to mentally abandon the two beats and get the message to their muscles to adapt to three beats, the music might suddenly change to five-beat time! At first, their arms and legs were all over the place and there would be groans of "Teacher, wait! wait!" But with practice, the movements became pleasant to do, and the children even thought up variations and enjoyed themselves.

Usually each child moved individually, but sometimes a pair would decide to act in unison, holding hands when the rhythm was in two-beat time; or they would try walking with their eyes closed. The only thing that was taboo was conversation.

Sometimes, when there was a Parent-Teacher Association meeting the mothers would peek in through the window. It was lovely to watch—each child moving arms and legs with ease, leaping about joyfully, in perfect time to the music.

Thus, the purpose of eurythmics was first to train both mind and body to be conscious of rhythm, thereby achieving harmony between the spirit and the flesh, and finally awakening the imagination and promoting creativity.

The day she arrived at the school for the very first time, Totto-chan had looked at the name on the gate and asked Mother, "What does Tomoe mean?"

The *tomoe* is an ancient comma-shaped symbol, and for his school the headmaster had adopted the traditional emblem consisting of two *tomoe*—one black and one white—united to form a perfect circle.

This symbolized his aim for the children: body and mind equally developed and in perfect harmony.

The headmaster had included eurythmics in his school curriculum because he felt it was bound to have good results and help the children's personalities to grow naturally, without being affected by too much adult interference.

The headmaster deplored contemporary education, with its emphasis on the written word, which tended to atrophy a child's sensual perception of nature and intuitive receptiveness to the still small voice of God, which is inspiration.

It was the poet Basho who wrote:

> Listen! a frog
>   Jumping into the silence
>   Of an ancient pond!

Yet the phenomenon of a frog jumping into a pond must have been seen by many others. Down through the ages and in the whole world, Watt and

Newton cannot have been the only ones to notice the steam from a boiling kettle or observe an apple fall.

Having eyes, but not seeing beauty; having ears, but not hearing music; having minds, but not perceiving truth; having hearts that are never moved and therefore never set on fire. These are the things to fear, said the headmaster.

As for Totto-chan, as she leaped and ran about in her bare feet, like Isadora Duncan, she was tremendously happy and could hardly believe that this was part of going to school!

🌷 *"The Only Thing I Want!"*

It was the first time Totto-chan had ever been to a temple fair. In the middle of Senzoku Pond, near her former school, was a small island with a shrine dedicated to Benten, the goddess of beauty and music. On the night of the annual fair, as she walked along the dimly lit road with Mother and Daddy, the night was suddenly ablaze with lights as they reached the fair. Totto-chan poked her head inside each of the little stalls. There were strange sounds everywhere—squeaks and sizzles and pops—and all sorts of enticing aromas. Everything was new and strange.

There were toy pipes, which you "smoked" by inhaling peppermint. They were decorated with pictures of cats and dogs and Betty Boop. There were lollipops and cotton candy. There were bamboo guns—tubes through which you pushed pieces of a certain kind of plant stem to make a loud pop.

A man by the side of the road was swallowing swords and eating glass; and there was a man selling a sort of powder you rubbed on the rim of a bowl to make it resound. There were magic golden rings that made money disappear, and pictures that developed when exposed to sunlight, and paper flowers that blossomed when dropped in a glass of water. As she walked along, her eyes darting this way and that, Totto-chan suddenly stopped.

"Oh, look!" she cried, seeing a box full of yellow baby chicks all cheeping away.

"I want one!" she said, pulling Mother and Daddy over. "Please buy me one! Please!"

The chicks all turned toward Totto-chan and raised their little heads to look at her, wiggling their tiny bottoms and cheeping even louder.

"Aren't they cute?" Totto-chan thought she had never seen anything quite so appealing in all her life, and she crouched down beside them.

"Please," she begged, looking up at Mother and Daddy. But to her amazement, her parents quickly tried to drag her away.

"But you said you'd buy me something, and this is the only thing I want!"

"No, dear," said Mother quietly. "These poor chicks are going to die very soon."

"Why?" asked Totto-chan, starting to cry.

Daddy drew her aside so the vendor couldn't hear, and explained, "They're cute now, Totsky, but they're terribly weak, and they won't live long. You'll only cry when it dies. That's why we don't want you to have one."

But Totto-chan had set her heart on having a baby chick, and wouldn't listen.

"I won't let it die! I'll look after it!"

Mother and Daddy kept trying to drag Totto-chan

away from the box, but she looked longingly at the chicks, and the chicks looked longingly at her, cheeping even louder still. Totto-chan had made up her mind that the only thing she wanted was a chick. She beseeched her parents, "Please, please buy me one."

Mother and Daddy were adamant.

"We don't want you to have one because it will only make you cry in the end."

Totto-chan burst out crying and started walking home with tears streaming down her cheeks. Once they were back on the dark road, she said, sobbing convulsively, "I've never wanted anything so much in my whole life. I'll never ask you to buy me anything ever again. Please buy me one of those chicks!"

Finally Mother and Daddy gave in.

It was like sunshine after rain. Totto-chan was all smiles now as she walked home carrying a small box containing two baby chicks.

The next day, Mother had the carpenter make a special slatted box, fitted with an electric light bulb to keep the chicks warm. Totto-chan watched the chicks all day long. The little yellow chicks were very cute. But, alas, on the fourth day one of them stopped moving and on the fifth day the other did, too. She stroked them and called to them, but they didn't give a single "cheep." She waited and waited but they never opened their eyes again. It was just as Mother and Daddy had said. Crying to herself, she dug a hole in the garden and buried the two little birds. And she laid a tiny flower over the spot. The box they had been in now seemed awfully big and empty. Catching sight of a tiny yellow feather in the corner of the box, she thought of the way the little chicks had cheeped when they saw her at the fair, and she clenched her teeth as she cried soundlessly.

She had never wanted anything so much in her life and now it was gone so soon. It was her first experience of loss and separation.

🪷 Their Worst Clothes

The headmaster was always asking parents to send their children to school at Tomoe in their worst clothes. He wanted them to wear their worst clothes so that it wouldn't matter if they got muddy and torn. He thought it a shame for children to worry about being scolded if their clothes got dirty or to hesitate joining in some game because their clothes might get torn. There were elementary schools near Tomoe where the girls were dressed in sailor-suit uniforms and the boys wore high-collared jackets with shorts. The Tomoe children came to school in their ordinary clothes, and they had their teachers' permission to play to their hearts' content without giving their clothes a thought. Trousers in those days weren't made of anything durable like today's jeans, so all the boys had patches on their trousers and the girls wore skirts or dresses made of the strongest material available.

Totto-chan's favorite pastime was crawling under the fences of other people's gardens and vacant lots, so it suited her very well not to have to think about her clothes. There were a lot of barbed-wire fences in those days, and some of them had wire right down to ground level. In order to get under one like that

84

you had to burrow like a dog. No matter how careful she was, Totto-chan would always manage to catch her dress on the barbs and tear it. Once, when she had on an old muslin dress that was really quite threadbare, the whole thing got shredded from top to bottom. Although it was old, she knew Mother was very fond of that dress, so Totto-chan racked her brains about what to say. She hadn't the heart to tell Mother she had torn it on barbed wire. She thought it would be better to think up a lie that would make it sound as if she couldn't help tearing it. She finally hit on the following story.

"As I was walking along the road," she lied, on arriving home, "a lot of children I didn't know threw knives at my back. That's why my dress got torn like this." But as she spoke she wondered how to answer further questions her mother might ask.

Thankfully, all her mother said was, "It must have been awful!"

Totto-chan heaved a sigh of relief. Mother obviously realized that under those circumstances she couldn't help getting Mother's favorite dress torn.

Naturally, Mother didn't believe her story about the knives. Knives thrown at her back would have injured her as well as tearing her dress, and Totto-chan didn't seem at all frightened by the incident. Mother realized at once it was a fabrication. However, it was unusual for Totto-chan to go to such lengths to make up an excuse. She realized Totto-chan must have felt badly about the dress and that pleased her. But there was something Mother had wanted to know for some time, and this seemed a good opportunity to find out.

"I can see how your dresses can get torn by knives

and things like that," said Mother, "but how do you manage to tear your panties too, day after day?"

Mother could never understand how Totto-chan's lace-trimmed panties got torn every day around the rear. She could see how panties could get muddy and worn thin by going down slides or falling on one's bottom, but how did they get torn to shreds?

Totto-chan thought about it for a while, then said, "You see, when you burrow under a fence you can't help catching your skirt as you go through, and your panties when you back out, and you have to do an 'Excuse me, may I come in?' and a 'Well, goodbye then' from one end of the fence to the other, so your panties and things are bound to tear."

Mother didn't really understand, but it sounded rather amusing.

"Is it fun?" she asked.

"Why don't you try it?" said Totto-chan, astonished at the question. "It's great fun and you'll tear your panties, too!"

The game that Totto-chan liked so much and found so thrilling went like this.

First you had to find a large vacant lot surrounded by a barbed-wire fence. "Excuse me, may I come in?" consisted of lifting up the spiked wire, digging a hole, and crawling under. Once inside you lifted up a neighboring bit of barbed wire and dug another hole, this time backing out saying, "Well, goodbye then." It became quite clear to Mother how Totto-chan's skirt got drawn up as she backed out causing her panties to catch on the barbed wire. The process would be repeated over and over again—burrowing under the wire with an "Excuse me, may I come in?" and then backing out through a fresh hole with a

"Well, goodbye then," tearing skirt and panties every time. Totto-chan happily zigzagged back and forth burrowing under the barbed-wire fence from one end to the other. No wonder her panties got torn.

To think that a game like that, which would only tire a grown-up and not be amusing at all, could be such fun to a child! Watching Totto-chan, with dirt in her hair and fingernails and even in her ears, Mother couldn't help feeling a little envious. And she couldn't help admiring the headmaster. His suggestion that the children wear clothes they could get as dirty as they liked was just another example of how well he understood them.

Takahashi

One morning, when they were all running about the school grounds, the headmaster said, "Here's a new friend for you. His last name is Takahashi. He'll be joining the first grade train."

The children, including Totto-chan, looked at Takahashi. He took off his hat and bowed, and said shyly, "How do you do?"

Totto-chan and her classmates were still quite small, being only in the first grade, but Takahashi, although he was a boy, was much smaller still, with short arms and legs. His hands, in which he held his hat, were small, too. But he had broad shoulders. He stood there looking forlorn.

"Let's talk to him," said Totto-chan to Miyo-chan and Sakko-chan. They went over to Takahashi. As they approached him he smiled affably, and they smiled back. He had big round eyes and looked as if he wanted to say something.

"Would you like to see the classroom in the train?" Totto-chan offered.

"Mm!" replied Takahashi, putting his hat back on his head.

Totto-chan was in a great hurry to show him the classroom and bounded over to the train, calling to him from the door, "Hurry up."

Takahashi seemed to be walking fast but was still a long way off.

"I'm coming," he said as he toddled along trying to run.

Totto-chan realized that while Takahashi didn't drag his leg like Yasuaki-chan, who had had polio, he was taking the same amount of time to get to the train. She quietly waited for him. Takahashi was running as fast as he could and there was no need to say, "Hurry," for he *was* hurrying. His legs were very short and he was bow-legged. The teachers and grown-ups knew that he had stopped growing. When he saw that Totto-chan was watching him, he tried to hurry faster, swinging his arms, and when he got to the door, he said, "You do run fast." Then he said, "I'm from Osaka."

"Osaka?" cried Totto-chan excitedly. Osaka was a dream city she had never seen. Mother's younger brother—her uncle—was a university student, and whenever he came to the house he used to take her head in both his hands and lift her up as high as he could, saying, "I'll show you Osaka. Can you see Osaka?"

It was just a game grown-ups used to play with children, but Totto-chan believed him. It stretched the skin of her face horribly and pulled her eyes out of shape and hurt her ears, but she would frantically look into the distance to try and see Osaka. But she never could. She always believed, however, that one day she would be able to see it, so whenever her uncle came, she would ask, "Show me Osaka." So Osaka had become the city of her dreams. And Takahashi came from there!

"Tell me about Osaka," she said to Takahashi.

"About Osaka?" he asked, smiling happily. His voice was clear and mature. Just then the bell rang for the first class.

"What a pity," said Totto-chan. Takahashi went in gaily, swinging the little body that was almost hidden by his bag, and sat down in the front row. Totto-chan hurriedly sat down next to him. She was glad you could sit anywhere you liked. She didn't want to leave him. Thus, Takahashi became one of her friends, too.

🌷 "Look before You Leap!"

On the way home from school, just as she had almost reached home, Totto-chan discovered something enticing by the side of the road. It was a huge pile of sand. How extraordinary to find sand there, so far from the sea! Was she dreaming? Totto-chan was thrilled. After a preliminary little hop she ran at great speed toward the pile of sand and leaped onto its summit. But it wasn't sand after all! Inside, it was a heap of prepared gray wall plaster. She sank into it with a "blop" and found herself covered in the gummy stuff right up to her chest, like a statue, complete with schoolbag and shoe bag. The more she struggled to get out, the more her feet slid about. Her shoes almost came off, and she had to be careful not to become buried in it completely. So there was nothing she could do but stay still, with her left arm stuck in the gooey mixture holding onto her shoe bag. One or two women whom she didn't know went by, and she said to them, "Excuse me . . ." in a small voice, but they all thought she was playing and smiled and went on their way.

As evening fell and it began to get dark, Mother came looking for her and was astonished to find Totto-chan's head sticking out of the pile. She found a pole and had Totto-chan hold one end of it while she pulled her out. She had first tried to pull her out by hand, but Mother's foot started to get stuck in the plaster.

Totto-chan was covered with gray plaster just like a wall.

"I thought I told you once before," said Mother, "when you see something that looks intriguing, don't jump on it straight away. Look before you leap!"

The "once before" that Mother was referring to happened during a lunch hour at school. Totto-chan was strolling along the little path behind the Assembly Hall when she saw a newspaper lying in the middle of the path. Thinking it would be fun to see if she could jump onto the newspaper, she took a few steps back, gave a little hop, and then, aiming for the center of the newspaper, ran toward it with tremendous speed and leaped onto it. But the newspaper had been left there by the janitor as a temporary covering for the cesspool opening mentioned before. He had gone away to do something and had laid the newspaper over the hole to keep the smell in because the concrete lid was off. Totto-chan fell right through and into the cesspool with a great big "plop." It was really awful. But fortunately they managed to make a clean little girl of Totto-chan again. That was the time Mother was talking about.

"No, I won't jump on anything again," said Totto-chan, quietly. Mother was relieved. But what Totto-chan said next made Mother think her relief was a bit premature.

"I won't jump onto a newspaper or a pile of sand ever again."

Mother was quite sure Totto-chan might easily take it into her head to jump onto something else.

The days were getting shorter and it was quite dark by the time they reached home.

❦ "And Then . . . Uh . . ."

Lunchtime at Tomoe had always been fun, but lately a new interest had been added.

The headmaster still inspected the lunchboxes of all fifty pupils to see if they had "something from the ocean and something from the hills"—and his wife with her two saucepans was ready to supply the missing elements from anyone's lunch—after which they would all sing "Chew, chew, chew it well, Everything you eat," followed by, "I gratefully partake." But from now on, after "I gratefully partake," someone had to give a little talk.

One day the headmaster said, "I think we all ought to learn how to speak better. What do you think? After this, while we are eating our lunch, let's have somebody different each day stand in the middle of the circle and tell us about something. How about that?"

Some children thought they weren't very good at speaking, but it would be fun to listen to others. Some thought it would be super to tell people things they knew. Totto-chan didn't know what she would talk about but was willing to give it a try. Most of the children were in favor of the idea so they decided to start the talks the next day.

Japanese children are usually taught at home not to talk at mealtimes. But as a result of his experience abroad, the headmaster used to encourage his pupils to take plenty of time over their meals and enjoy conversation.

Besides that, he thought it was essential for them to learn how to get up in front of people and express their ideas clearly and freely without being embarrassed, so he decided it was time to put this theory into practice.

After the children had agreed to the idea, this is what he told them. Totto-chan listened attentively.

"You needn't worry about trying to be a good speaker," he said. "And you can talk about anything you like. You can talk about things you'd like to do. Anything. At any rate, let's give it a try."

The order of speakers was decided upon. And it was also decided that whoever was going to speak that day would eat lunch quickly, straight away after the song was over.

The children soon discovered that unlike talking to two or three friends during lunch hour, standing up in the middle of the whole school needed a good deal of courage and was quite difficult. Some children were so shy at first that they just giggled. One boy had gone to a lot of effort and prepared a talk only to forget all of it the moment he stood up. He repeated several times his fine-sounding title, "Why Frogs Jump Sideways," then started off with, "When it rains . . ." but got no further. Finally he said, "That's all," bowed, and went back to his seat.

Totto-chan's turn hadn't come yet, but she decided that when it did she would tell her favorite story, "The Prince and the Princess." Everyone knew it, and whenever she wanted to tell it during breaks, the children would say, "We're tired of that one."

But all the same, she decided, that was the story she was going to tell.

The new scheme was beginning to work rather well when, one day, the child whose turn it was to give a talk firmly refused.

"I have nothing to say," the boy declared.

Totto-chan was amazed to think that anyone could possibly have nothing to say. But that boy just didn't. The headmaster went over to the boy's desk with its empty lunchbox.

"So you have nothing to say," he said.

"Nothing."

The boy wasn't trying to be clever, or anything like that. He honestly couldn't think of anything to talk about.

The headmaster threw back his head and laughed, heedless of the gaps in his teeth.

"Let's try and find you something to say."

"Find me something?" The boy seemed startled.

The headmaster got the boy to stand in the center of the ring while he sat down at the boy's desk.

"Try and remember," he said, "what you did this morning after you got up and before you came to school. What did you do first?"

"Well," said the boy and then just scratched his head.

"Fine," said the headmaster, "You've said, 'Well.' You did have something to say. What did you do after 'well?'"

"Well, . . . uh . . . I got up," he said, scratching his head some more.

Totto-chan and the others were amused, but listened attentively. The boy went on, "Then, uh . . ." He scratched his head again. The headmaster sat patiently watching the boy, with a smile on his face and his hands clasped on the desk. Then he said, "That's splendid. That will do. You got up this morning. You've made everyone understand that. You don't have to be amusing or make people laugh to be a good speaker. The important thing is that you said you hadn't anything to talk about and you did find something to say."

But the boy didn't sit down. He said in a very loud voice, "And then . . . uh . . ."

All the children leaned forward. The boy took a deep breath and went on, "And then . . . uh . . . Mother . . . uh . . . she said, 'Brush your teeth' . . . uh . . . so I brushed my teeth."

The headmaster clapped. Everyone else clapped, too. Whereupon the boy, in an even louder voice than before, went on again, "And then . . . uh . . ."

The children stopped clapping and listened with bated breath, leaning forward even more.

Finally, the boy said, triumphantly, "And then . . . uh . . . I came to school."

One of the older boys leaned forward so far he lost his balance and hit his face on his lunchbox. But everyone was terribly pleased that the boy had found something to talk about.

The headmaster clapped vigorously, and Totto-chan and the others did, too. Even "And then . . . uh . . . ," who was still standing in their midst, clapped. The Assembly Hall was filled with the sound of clapping.

Even when he was a grown man that boy probably never forgot the sound of that applause.

"We Were Only Playing!"

Totto-chan had a terrible accident. It happened after she got home from school, while she and Rocky were playing "wolf" in her room before dinner.

They had begun by playing a game where you rolled toward each other from opposite sides of the room, ending in a brief tussle when you bumped into each other. They played this several times and then

decided to try something a little more complicated—although it was Totto-chan, of course, who did
the deciding. The idea was that when they met
in the middle of the room after rolling toward
each other, the one who made the fiercer wolf face at
the other would be the winner. Rocky was a German
shepherd, so it wasn't hard for him to look like a
wolf. All he had to do was point his ears, open his
mouth, and bare all his teeth. He could make his
eyes look pretty fierce, too. It was a little more difficult for Totto-chan. She would hold both hands up
on either side of her head to look like ears, open her
mouth and eyes as wide as she could, make growling
noises, and pretend to bite Rocky. At first, Rocky
played the game very well. But he was a puppy, and
after a while, he forgot it was just a game and suddenly bit Totto-chan in earnest.

Although still a puppy, Rocky was almost twice as
big as Totto-chan and had sharp, pointed teeth, so
before she realized what was happening her right ear
was dangling from her head and blood was streaming down.

Hearing her screams, Mother came rushing from
the kitchen to find Totto-chan in the corner of the
room with Rocky, holding her right ear with both
hands. Her dress was splattered with blood. Daddy,
who had been practicing the violin in the living
room, came rushing in, too. Rocky seemed to realize
he had done something terrible. His tail hung between his legs and he looked pathetically at Totto-
chan.

The only thing Totto-chan could think of was
what would she do if Mother and Daddy got so
angry with Rocky they got rid of him or gave him

away? That would have been the saddest and most dreadful thing as far as she was concerned. So she crouched down beside Rocky, holding her right ear and crying out repeatedly, "Don't scold Rocky! Don't scold Rocky!"

Mother and Daddy were more interested in seeing what had happened to her ear and tried to pull her hands away. Totto-chan wouldn't let go and shouted, "It doesn't hurt! Don't be cross with Rocky! Don't be cross!" Totto-chan truly wasn't conscious of the pain at the time. All she could think of was Rocky.

Blood kept trickling down, and Mother and Daddy eventually realized that Rocky must have bitten her. But they assured Totto-chan they wouldn't be cross with him, and the child finally removed her hands. When she saw Totto-chan's ear dangling, Mother screamed. Daddy carried his little girl to the doctor's with Mother leading the way. Luckily, because it was treated in time, the doctor was able to fasten the ear back, just as it was before, to her parents' great relief. But the only thing Totto-chan was concerned about, however, was whether Mother and Daddy would keep their promise not to scold Rocky.

Totto-chan went home all bandaged from the top of her head to her chin, looking just like a white rabbit. In spite of his promise not to scold Rocky, Daddy felt very inclined to admonish the dog in some way. But Mother gave him a look with her eyes as much as to say, "Please keep your promise," and Daddy reluctantly did so.

Totto-chan rushed into the house, anxious to let Rocky know, as soon as possible, that everything was all right, and nobody was cross any more. But she couldn't find Rocky anywhere. For the first time, Totto-chan cried. She hadn't cried at the doctor's, she had been so afraid that if she did, it would increase her parents' anger with the dog. But there was no stopping her tears now. As she cried, she called, "Rocky! Rocky! Where are you?"

After calling several more times, her tear-stained face lifted into a smile as a familiar brown back emerged slowly from behind the sofa. Going up to Totto-chan, he gently licked the good ear that was just visible among the bandages. Totto-chan put her arms around Rocky's neck and sniffed inside his ears. Mother and Daddy used to say they were smelly, but how she loved that dear familiar odor.

Rocky and Totto-chan were tired and very sleepy.

The end-of-summer moon looked down from above the garden on the little bandaged girl and the dog who never wanted to play "wolf" again. The two were even better friends now than they had been before.

🌷 Sports Day

Tomoe's Sports Day was held every year on the third of November. The headmaster had decided on that day after a lot of research, in which he found out that the third of November was the autumn day on which it had rained the fewest times. Perhaps it was due to his skill in collecting weather data, or perhaps it was just that the sun and clouds heeded his desire—that no rain should mar the Sports Day so anticipated by the children, who had decorated the school grounds the day before and made all sorts of preparations. Whatever it was, it was almost uncanny the way it never rained on that day.

As all kinds of things were done differently at Tomoe, its Sports Day, too, was unique. The only sports events that were the same as at other elementary schools were the Tug of War and the Three-Legged Race. All the rest had been invented by the headmaster. Requiring no special or elaborate equipment, they made use of familiar everyday school things.

For instance, there was the Carp Race. Large tubular cloth streamers, shaped and painted like carp—the kind that are flown from poles in May for Boys' Day Festival—were laid in the middle of the school grounds. At the signal, the children had to start running toward the carp streamers and crawl through them from the mouth end to the tail end and then run back to the starting point. There were only three carp—one red and two blue—so three children raced at a time. The race looked easy but was quite difficult. It was dark inside, and the carp were long, so you could easily lose your sense of direction. Some children, including Totto-chan, kept coming out of the mouth, only to realize their mistake and hurriedly burrow inside again. It was terribly funny to watch because the children crawling backward and forward inside made the carp wriggle as if they were alive.

There was another event called Find-A-Mother Race. At the signal the children had to run toward a wooden ladder propped up on its side, crawl through it between the rungs, take an envelope from a basket, open it, and if the paper inside said, for instance, "Sakko-chan's mother," they would have to find her in the crowd of spectators, take her hand, and return together to the finishing line. One had to ease oneself through the ladder with catlike grace or one's bottom could get stuck. Besides that, a child might know well enough who Sakko-chan's mother was, but if the paper read "Miss Oku's sister," or "Mr. Tsue's mother," or Mrs. Kuninori's son," whom one had never met, one had to go to the spectators' section and call in a loud voice, "Miss Oku's sister!" It took courage. Children who were lucky and picked their own mothers would jump up and down shouting, "Mother! Mother! Hurry!" The spectators, too, had to be alert for this event. There was no telling when their names might be called, and they would have to be ready to get up from the bench or from the mat where they were sitting, excuse themselves, and wend their way out as fast as they could to where someone's child was waiting, take his or her hand, and go running off. So when a child arrived and stopped in front of the grown-ups, even the fathers held their breath, wondering who was going to be called. There was little time for idle chit-chat or nibbling food. The grown-ups had to take part in events almost as much as the children.

The headmaster and other teachers joined the children in the two teams for the Tug of War, pulling and shouting, "Heave-ho, heave-ho!" while handicapped children, like Yasuaki-chan, who couldn't pull, had the task of keeping their eyes on the handkerchief tied to the center of the rope to see who was winning.

The final Relay Race involving the whole school was also different at Tomoe. No one had to run very far. All one had to do was run up and down the semicircular flight of concrete steps leading to the Assembly Hall. At first glance it looked absurdly easy, but the steps were unusually shallow and close together, and as no one was allowed to take more than one step at a time, it was quite difficult if you were tall or had large feet. The familiar steps, bounded up each day at lunchtime, took on a fresh, fun aspect on Sports Day, and the children hurried up and down them shrieking gaily. To anyone watching from afar, the scene would have looked like a beautiful kaleidoscope. Counting the top one there were eight steps in all.

The first Sports Day for Totto-chan and her classmates was a fine day just as the headmaster had hoped. The decorations of paper chains and gold stars made by the children the day before and the phonograph records of rousing marches made it seem like a festival.

Totto-chan wore navy blue shorts and a white blouse, although she would have preferred to wear athletic bloomers. She longed to wear them. One day after school the headmaster had been giving a class in eurythmics to some kindergarten teachers, and Totto-chan was very taken with the bloomers some of the women were wearing. What she liked about them was that when the women stamped their feet on the ground, their lower thighs showing beneath the bloomers rippled in such a lovely grown-up way. She ran home and got out her shorts and put them on and stamped on the floor. But her thin, childish thighs didn't ripple at all. After trying several times, she came to the conclusion it was because of what those ladies had been wearing. She asked what they were and Mother explained they were athletic bloomers. She told Mother she definitely wanted to wear bloomers on Sports Day, but they couldn't find any in a small size. That was why Totto-chan had to make do with shorts, which didn't produce any ripples, alas.

Something amazing happened on Sports Day. Takahashi, who had the shortest arms and legs and was the smallest in the school, came first in everything. It was unbelievable. While the others were still creeping about inside the carp, Takahashi was through it in a flash, and while the others only had their heads through the ladder, he was already out of it and running several yards ahead. As for the Relay Race up the Assembly Hall steps, while the others were clumsily negotiating them a step at a time, Takahashi—his short legs moving like pistons —was up them in one spurt and down again like a speeded-up movie.

"We've got to try and beat Takahashi," they all said.

Determined to beat him, the children did their utmost, but try as they might, Takahashi won every time. Totto-chan tried hard, too, but she never managed to beat Takahashi. They could outrun him on the straight stretches, but lost to him over the difficult bits.

Takahashi went up to collect his prizes, looking happy and as proud as Punch. He was first in everything so he collected prize after prize. Everyone watched enviously.

"I'll beat Takahashi next year!" said each child to himself. But every year it was Takahashi who turned out to be the star athlete.

Now the prizes, too, were typical of the headmaster. First Prize might be a giant radish; Second Prize, two burdock roots; Third Prize, a bundle of spinach. Things like that. Until she was much older Totto-chan thought all schools gave vegetables for Sports Day prizes.

In those days, most schools gave notebooks, pencils, and erasers for prizes. The Tomoe children didn't know that, but they weren't happy about the vegetables. Totto-chan, for instance, who got some burdock roots and some onions, was embarrassed about having to carry them on the train. Additional prizes were given for various things, so at the end of Sports Day all the children at Tomoe had some sort of vegetable. Now, why should children be embarrassed about going home from school with vegetables? No one minded being sent to buy vegetables by his mother, but they apparently felt it would look odd carrying vegetables home from school.

A fat boy who won a cabbage didn't know what to do with it.

"I don't want to be seen carrying this," he said. "I think I'll throw it away."

The headmaster must have heard about their complaints for he went over to the children with their carrots and radishes and things.

"What's the matter? Don't you want them?" he asked. Then he went on, "Get your mothers to cook them for you for dinner tonight. They're vegetables you earned yourselves. You have provided food for your families by your own efforts. How's that? I'll bet it tastes good!"

Of course, he was right. It was the first time in her life, for instance, that Totto-chan had ever provided anything for dinner.

"I'll get Mother to make spicy burdock!" she told the headmaster. "I haven't decided yet what to ask her to make with the onions."

Whereupon the others all began thinking up menus, too, describing them to the headmaster.

"Good! So now you've got the idea," he said, smiling so happily his cheeks became quite flushed. He was probably thinking how nice it would be if the children and their families ate the vegetables while talking over the Sports Day events.

No doubt he was thinking especially of Takahashi—whose dinner table would be overflowing with First Prizes—and hoping the boy would remember his pride and happiness at winning those First Prizes before developing an inferiority complex about his size and the fact he would never grow. And maybe, who knows, the headmaster had thought up those singularly Tomoe-type events just so Takahashi would come first in them.

The Poet Issa

The children liked to call the headmaster "Issa Kobayashi." They even made up affectionate verses about him like the following:

> Issa Kobayashi!
>   Issa's our Old Man
>   With his bald head!

That was because the headmaster's family name was Kobayashi, the same as that of the famous nineteenth-century poet Issa Kobayashi, whose haiku he loved. He quoted Issa's haiku so often, the children felt as if Issa Kobayashi was just as much their friend as Sosaku Kobayashi, their headmaster.

The headmaster loved Issa's haiku because they were so true and dealt with the ordinary things in life. At a time when there must have been thousands of haiku poets, Issa created a world of his own that nobody was able to imitate. The headmaster admired his verses with their almost childlike simplicity. So at every opportunity, he would teach his pupils verses by Issa, which they would learn by heart, such as:

> Lean Frog,
>> Don't you surrender!
>> Here's Issa by you.

> Fledgling Sparrows!
>> Make way, make way,
>> Way for the noble Horse!

> Spare the Fly!
>> Wringing his hands, wringing his feet,
>> He implores your mercy!

The headmaster once improvised a melody for one, and they all sang it.

106

The headmaster often held haiku classes, although they were not a formal part of the curriculum.

Totto-chan's first effort at composing haiku described her favorite comic-strip character Norakuro, a stray black dog who had joined the army as a private and gradually earned promotion in spite of the ups and downs in his career. It ran in a popular boy's magazine.

> Straydog Black sets off
> For the Continent, now that
> He has been demobilized.

The headmaster had said "Try making up an honest, straightforward haiku about something that is in your thoughts."

You couldn't call Totto-chan's a proper haiku. But it did show what sort of thing impressed her in those days. Her haiku didn't quite conform to the proper 5-7-5 syllable form. Hers was 5-7-7. But then, Issa's one about the fledgling sparrows in Japanese was 5-8-7, so Totto-chan thought it would be all right.

During their walks to Kuhonbutsu Temple, or when it rained and they couldn't play outdoors but gathered in the Assembly Hall, Tomoe's Issa Kobayashi would tell the children about haiku. He also used haiku to illustrate his own thoughts about life and nature.

Some of Issa's haiku might have been written especially for Tomoe.

> The snow thaws—
> And suddenly the whole village
> Is full of children!

Totto-chan found some money for the first time in her life. It happened during the train ride going home from school. She got on the Oimachi train at Jiyugaoka. Before the train reached the next station, Midorigaoka, there was a sharp curve, and the train always leaned over with a great creaking. Totto-chan would brace herself with her feet so she wouldn't go "Oops." She always stood by the right-hand door at the rear of the train, facing the way the train was going. She stood there because the platform at her own station was on the right-hand side and that door was nearest the exit.

That day, as the train leaned over, creaking as usual as it went around the curve, Totto-chan noticed something that looked like money lying near her feet. She had picked up something once before that she thought was money but it turned out to be a button, so she thought she had better have a good look this time. When the train straightened out, she put her head right down and looked at it carefully. It was definitely money—a five-sen coin. She thought somebody nearby must have dropped it and it had come rolling toward her when the train leaned over. But nobody was standing anywhere near Totto-chan.

What should she do, she wondered? Just then she remembered someone saying that when you found money, you should hand it to a policeman. But there wasn't a policeman on the train, was there?

Just then, the conductor's compartment opened and the conductor entered the car in which Totto-chan was. Totto-chan herself didn't know what made her do it, but she put her right foot over the five-sen piece. The conductor knew her and smiled. But Totto-chan couldn't smile back wholeheartedly because she felt guilty about what was under her right foot. All she could manage was a weak grin. At that moment the train stopped at Ookayama, the station before hers, and the doors on the left side opened. An unusual number of people got on and Totto-chan was pushed and jostled. Totto-chan had no intention of moving her right foot and desperately stood her ground. While doing so, she thought out her plan. When she got off the train she would take the money and hand it to a policeman. Then another thought occurred to her. If any grown-ups saw her pick up the coin from under her foot, they might think she was a thief! In those days you could buy a small packet of caramels or a bar of chocolate for five sen. So while it wouldn't seem like much of a sum to a grown-up, it was a large amount of money as far as Totto-chan was concerned, and she became quite worried about it.

"That's it!" she said to herself. "I'll say quietly, 'Oh, I've dropped some money. I must pick it up.' Then everyone's bound to think it's mine!"

But immediately another problem occurred to her, "What if I say that and everyone looks at me and someone says, 'That's mine!' What will I do?"

After turning over lots of ideas in her mind, she decided the best thing to do would be to crouch down as the train neared her station, pretending to tie her shoelace, and pick up the money secretly. It worked. When she stepped onto the platform, damp with perspiration and clutching the five-sen piece, she felt exhausted. The police station was a long way off and if she went and handed in the money she would get home late and Mother would be worried. She thought hard as she clumped down the stairs, and this is what she decided to do.

"I'll put it in a secret place, and then tomorrow I'll take it to school and ask everyone's advice. I ought to show it to them anyway, because nobody else has ever found any money."

She wondered where to hide the money. If she took it home, Mother might ask about it, so it would have to be hidden somewhere else.

She climbed into a thicket near the station. Nobody could see her there, and no one was likely to climb in, so it seemed pretty safe. She dug a tiny hole with a stick, dropped the precious five-sen coin into it, and covered it with earth. She found an oddly shaped stone and put it on top as a marker. Then she ran home at tremendous speed.

Most nights Totto-chan would stay up talking about school until Mother announced, "Time to go to bed." But that night, she didn't talk much and went to bed early.

The following morning she awoke with the feeling there was something terribly important she had to do. Suddenly remembering her secret treasure, she was very happy.

Leaving home earlier than usual, she raced Rocky to the thicket and scrambled in.

"It's here! It's here!"

The stone marker was just as she had left it.

"I'll show you something lovely," she said to Rocky, removing the stone and digging carefully. But strangely enough, the five-sen coin had disappeared! She had never been so surprised. Did someone see her hide it, she wondered, or had the stone moved? She dug all around, but the five-sen piece was nowhere to be found. She was very disappointed not to be able to show it to her friends at Tomoe, but more than that she couldn't get over the mysteriousness of it.

Thereafter, every time she passed by she would climb into the thicket and dig, but never again did she see that five-sen piece.

"Perhaps a mole took it?" she would think. Or, "Did I dream it?" Or, "Maybe God saw me hide it." But no matter how much she thought about it, it was very strange, indeed. A very mysterious happening that she would never forget.

☙ Talking with Your Hands

One afternoon, near the ticket gate at Jiyugaoka Station, two boys and one girl slightly older than Tottochan were standing together, looking as if they were playing "stone, paper, scissors." But she noticed they were making a lot more signs with their fingers than usual. What fun it looked! She went closer so she could get a better view. They seemed to be holding a conversation without making a sound. One would make a lot of signs with his hands, then another who was watching would immediately make a lot more different signs. Then the third would do a few, and they would all burst out laughing, without making much sound. They seemed to be enjoying themselves. After watching them for some time, Tottochan came to the conclusion they were talking with their hands.

"I wish I could talk with my hands, too," she thought enviously. She considered going over and

111

joining them, but she didn't know how to ask them with her hands. And besides, they weren't Tomoe students, so it might be rude, so she just went on watching them until they left for the Toyoko train platform.

"Someday I'm going to learn how to talk to people with my hands," she decided.

But Totto-chan didn't know yet about deaf people, or that those children went to the municipal deaf and dumb school in Oimachi, the last stop of the train she took to school each day.

Totto-chan just thought there was something rather beautiful about the way those children watched each other's fingers with shining eyes, and she wanted to make friends with them someday.

The Forty-seven Ronin

While Mr. Kobayashi's system of education was unique, he had been influenced a great deal by ideas from Europe and other foreign countries, as we can see from Tomoe's eurythmics, its mealtime customs, its school walks, and the lunchtime song that was sung to the tune of "Row, Row, Row Your Boat."

The headmaster's right-hand man—at an ordinary school he would be the vice-principal—Mr. Maruyama, was in many ways the exact opposite of Mr. Kobayashi. Like his name, meaning "round hill," his head was completely round, without a single hair on top, but with a fringe of white hair at the back at ear level. He wore round glasses, and his cheeks were bright red. He not only looked quite different from Mr. Kobayashi, but he used to recite classical Chinese-style poems in a solemn voice.

On the morning of December fourteenth, when the children were all assembled at school, Mr. Maruyama made the following announcement:

"This is the day, nearly two and a half centuries ago, that the Forty-seven Ronin executed their famous vendetta. So we are going to walk to the temple of Sengakuji and pay our respects at their graves. Your parents have already been told."

The headmaster did not oppose Mr. Maruyama's plan. What Mr. Kobayashi thought of it the parents didn't know, but they knew if he didn't oppose it, he must have approved of it, and the prospect of Tomoe children visiting the tombs of the Forty-seven Ronin was indeed an intriguing one.

Before they left, Mr. Maruyama told the children the story of the famous Forty-seven—how Lord Asano's brave and loyal men had plotted for almost two years to avenge the honor of their dead master, who had been so grievously wronged. Besides the Forty-seven there was a courageous merchant called Rihei Amanoya. It was he who supplied the weapons, and when he was arrested by the officials of the shogun he declared, "I, Rihei Amanoya, am a man" and refused to confess or give away a single secret. The children didn't understand much of the story, but they were excited about missing classes and going for a walk to a place much further away than Kuhonbutsu Temple—and a picnic lunch.

Taking their leave of the headmaster and the other teachers all fifty students started off, led by Mr. Maruyama. Here and there in the line children's voices could be heard declaiming, "I, Rihei Amanoya, am a man." Girls declaimed it, too, causing passersby to turn their heads and laugh. It was about

113

seven miles to Sengakuji, but motor vehicles were scarce, the December sky was blue, and, to the children strolling along firing a constant barrage of, "I, Rihei Amanoya, am a man," the way did not seem long at all.

When they got to Sengakuji, Mr. Maruyama gave each child a stick of incense and a few flowers. The temple was smaller than Kuhonbutsu, but there were lots of graves all in a row. The thought that this place was sacred to the memory of the Forty-seven Ronin made Totto-chan feel very solemn as she offered the incense and the flowers, and she bowed

silently, imitating Mr. Maruyama. A hush fell upon the children. It was unusual for Tomoe pupils to be so quiet. The smoke from the incense sticks placed before each tomb drifted up, drawing pictures in the sky for a long, long time.

After that, the smell of incense always made the children think of Mr. Maruyama and of Rihei Amanoya. It also became for them the aroma of silence.

The children may not have understood all about the Forty-seven Ronin, but for Mr. Maruyama, who spoke of these men with such fervor, the children felt almost as much respect and affection as for Mr. Kobayashi, although in a different way. Totto-chan loved his little eyes that peered from behind the thick lenses of his glasses, and his gentle voice that didn't seem to go with such a large body.

"MaSOW-chaan!"

On her way to and from the station, Totto-chan used to pass a tenement where some Koreans lived. Totto-chan, of course, didn't know they were Koreans. The only thing she knew about them was that there was a woman there who wore her hair parted down the middle and drawn back into a bun, and who was rather plump and wore white rubber shoes that were pointed in front like little boats. She wore a dress with a long skirt and a ribbon tied in a big bow on the front of her short blouse, and always seemed to be looking for her son, calling out, "MaSOW-chaan!" She was always calling his name. And instead of pronouncing it "Ma-sa-o-chan," as people normally would, she stressed the second syllable and drew out the "chan" in a high-pitched voice that sounded sad to Totto-chan.

The tenement was right beside the Oimachi train tracks on a small embankment. Totto-chan knew who Masao-chan was. He was a little bigger than she was and probably in second grade, although she didn't know which school he went to. He had untidy hair and always had a dog with him. One day, as Totto-chan was walking home past the embankment, Masao-chan was standing on top of it with his feet apart and his hands on his hips, in an arrogant posture.

"Korean!" he shouted at Totto-chan.

His voice was scathing and full of hatred. Totto-chan was scared. She had never done anything mean to him, or even spoken to him for that matter, so she was startled when he yelled at her from above in such a spiteful way.

When she got home she told Mother about it. "Masao-chan called me a Korean," she said. Mother put her hand to her mouth and Totto-chan saw her eyes fill with tears. Totto-chan was perplexed, thinking it must be something very bad. Mother didn't stop to wipe away her tears, and the tip of her nose was red. "Poor child!" she said. "People must call him 'Korean! Korean!' so often that he thinks it's a nasty word. He probably doesn't understand what it means because he's still young. He thinks it's like *baka*, which people say when they mean 'you fool.' Masao-chan has probably had 'Korean' said to him so often he wanted to say something nasty to somebody else, so he called you a Korean. Why are people so cruel?"

Drying her eyes, Mother said to Totto-chan very

116

slowly, "You're Japanese and Masao-chan comes from a country called Korea. But he's a child, just like you. So, Totto-chan, dear, don't ever think of people as different. Don't think, 'That person's a Japanese, or this person's a Korean.' Be nice to Masao-chan. It's so sad that some people think other people aren't nice just because they're Koreans."

It was all rather difficult for Totto-chan to understand, but what she did understand was that Masao-chan was a little boy whom people spoke ill of for no reason at all. That must be why his mother was always searching for him so anxiously, she thought. So next morning, as she passed the embankment and heard his mother calling out, "MaSOW-chaan" in her shrill voice, she wondered where he could be, and made up her mind that even though she herself wasn't a Korean, if Masao-chan called her that again, she would reply, "We're all children! We're all the same," and she'd try to make friends with him.

Masao-chan's mother's voice, with its combination of irritation and anxiety, had a special quality of its own that seemed to linger in the air for a long time, until it was drowned by the sound of a passing train.

"MaSOW-chaan!"

Once you heard the sad, tearful sound of that voice you could never forget it.

Pigtails

About that time, Totto-chan had two great ambitions. One was to wear athletic bloomers, and the other was to braid her hair. Watching older schoolgirls with long braids in the train, she decided she wanted to wear her hair that way, too. While the rest of the little girls in her class wore their hair short, with bangs, Totto-chan wore hers longer, parted at the side and tied with a ribbon. Mother liked it that way, and besides, Totto-chan wanted it to grow so she could wear pigtails.

Finally, one day she got Mother to braid her hair into two little pigtails. With the ends secured by rubber bands and tied with slender ribbons, she felt like an older student. When she looked at herself in the mirror, she realized that, unlike the girls in the train, her braids were thin and short and really looked like pigs' tails, but she ran to Rocky and held them up proudly for him to see. Rocky blinked once or twice.

"I wish I could braid *your* hair, too," she said.

When she got on the train she held her head as still as she could for fear the braids might come undone. "How nice it would be," she thought, "if someone noticed them on the train and said, 'What lovely braids!' " But nobody did. When she got to school, however, Miyo-chan, Sakko-chan, and Keiko Aoki, who were all in her class, exclaimed in unison, "Oooh! Pigtails!" and she was awfully pleased and let the girls feel them.

None of the boys seemed impressed. But all of a sudden, after lunch, a boy from her class named Oe said in a loud voice, "Wow! Totto-chan's got a new hairdo!"

Totto-chan was thrilled to think one of the boys had noticed, and said proudly, "They're pigtails."

Whereupon he came over, took hold of them with both hands, and said, "I'm tired. I think I'll hang onto them for a while. Gee, they're much nicer than the hand straps on the train!" But that wasn't the end of her trouble.

Oe was twice as big as skinny little Totto-chan. In fact, he was the biggest and fattest boy in the class. So when he pulled on her pigtails she staggered and fell smack on her bottom. To have them called hand straps was hurtful enough, without being dragged to the ground as well. But when Oe tried to pull her up by her pigtails, with a "Heave-ho, heave-ho!" just like at the Sports Day Tug of War, Totto-chan burst into tears.

To Totto-chan, pigtails were the emblem of an older girl. She had expected everyone to be very polite to her because of them. Crying, she ran to the headmaster's office. When he heard her knocking on the door, sobbing, he opened it, and bent down as usual so their faces were level.

"What's the matter?" he asked.

After checking to see if her pigtails were still properly braided, she said, "Oe pulled them, saying 'Heave-ho, heave-ho.' "

The headmaster looked at her hair. In contrast to her tearful face, her little pigtails looked as if they were dancing gaily. He sat down and had Totto-chan sit down, too, facing him. As usual, heedless of his missing teeth, he grinned.

"Don't cry," he said. "Your hair looks lovely."

"Do you like it?" she asked, rather shyly, raising her tear-stained face.

"It's terrific!" he said.

Totto-chan stopped crying, and got down from her chair saying, "I won't cry any more even if Oe says 'Heave-ho.' "

The headmaster nodded approval with a grin.

Totto-chan smiled, too. Her smiling face suited her pigtails. Bowing to the headmaster, she ran back and began playing with the other children.

She had almost forgotten about having cried when she saw Oe standing in front of her, scratching his head.

"I'm sorry I pulled them," he said in a loud, flat voice. "I've been scolded by the headmaster. He said you've got to be nice to girls. He said to be gentle with girls and look after them."

Totto-chan was somewhat amazed. She had never heard anyone before say you had to be nice to girls. Boys were always the important ones. In the families she knew where there were lots of children, it was always the boys who were served first at meals and at snack time, and when girls spoke, their mothers would say, "Little girls should be seen and not heard."

In spite of all that, the headmaster had told Oe that girls should be looked after. It seemed strange to Totto-chan. And then she thought how nice that was. It was nice to be looked after.

As for Oe, it was a shock. Fancy being told to be gentle and nice to girls! Moreover, it was the first and last time at Tomoe that he was ever scolded by the headmaster, and he never forgot that day.

"Thank You"

New Year's vacation drew near. Unlike summer vacation, the children didn't gather at school at all but spent the whole time with their families.

"I'm going to spend New Year's with my grandfather in Kyushu," Migita kept telling everyone, while Tai-chan, who liked doing science experiments, said, "I'm going with my older brother to visit a physics laboratory." He was looking forward to it. "Well, I'll be seeing you," each said, telling one another their plans as they parted company.

Totto-chan went skiing with Daddy and Mother. Daddy's friend Hideo Saito, the cellist and conductor in the same orchestra, had a beautiful house in the Shiga Highlands. They used to stay with him there every winter, and Totto-chan had started learning how to ski from the time she was in kindergarten.

You took a horse-drawn sleigh from the station to the skiing area—a pure white snowscape, unbroken by ski lifts or anything but the stumps of trees here and there. For people who didn't have a house like Mr. Saito's to go to, Mother said there was only one Japanese-style inn and one Western-style hotel. But, interestingly, lots of foreigners went there.

For Totto-chan, this year was different from the year before. She was now a first grade pupil at elementary school, and also she knew one bit of English. Daddy had taught her how to say, "Thank you."

Foreigners who passed Totto-chan standing on the snow in her skis always used to say something. It was probably, "Isn't she sweet," or something like that, but Totto-chan didn't understand. And until this year she hadn't been able to reply, but from now on she tried bobbing her head and saying, "Thank you."

That made the foreigners smile even more and say something to each other. Sometimes a lady would bend down and put her cheek against Totto-chan's cheek, or a gentleman would hug her. Totto-chan thought it was great fun to be able to make such good friends with people just by saying, "Thank you."

One day a nice young man came over to Totto-chan and gestured as much as to say, "Would you like a ride on the front of my skis?" Daddy told her she could.

"Thank you," replied Totto-chan, and the man had her sit down by his feet on his skis with her knees drawn up. Then, keeping both his skis together, he skied with Totto-chan down the gentlest and longest slope at Shiga Highlands. They went like the wind, and as the air rushed past her ears it made a whistling sound. Totto-chan hugged her knees tightly taking care not to fall forward. It was a bit scary, but tremendous fun. When they came to a halt, the people who were watching clapped. Getting up from the man's skis, Totto-chan bowed her head slightly to the onlookers, and said, "Thank you." They clapped all the more.

Much later on she learned that the man's name was Schneider, and that he was a world-famous skier, who always used a pair of silver ski poles. But that day, what she liked about him was that after they had skied down the slope, and everybody had clapped, he crouched down beside her and, taking her hand, he looked at her as if she was somebody important and said, "Thank you." He didn't treat her like a child, but like a real grown-up lady. When he bent down, Totto-chan knew in her heart, instinctively, that he was a gentleman. And beyond him, the snow-white landscape seemed to go on forever.

When the children returned to school after the winter vacation, they discovered something wonderful and new, and greeted their discovery with shouts of joy. Opposite the row of classroom cars stood the new car, beside the flower bed by the Assembly Hall. In their absence it had become a library! Ryo-chan, the janitor, whom everyone respected and who could do all sorts of things, had obviously been working terribly hard. He had put up lots and lots of shelves in the car, and they were filled with rows of books of all kinds and colors. There were desks and chairs, too, where you could sit and read.

"This is your library," the headmaster said. "Any of these books may be read by anyone. You needn't fear that some books are reserved for certain grades, or anything like that. You can come in here any time you like. If you want to borrow a book and take it home, you may. When you've read it, be sure and bring it back! And if you've got any books at home you think the others would like to read, I'd be delighted if you'd bring them here. At any rate, please do as much reading as you can!"

"Let's make the first class today a library class!" cried the children, unanimously.

"Is that what you'd like to do?" said the headmaster, smiling happily to see them so excited. "All right, then, why not?"

Whereupon, the whole student body of Tomoe —all fifty children—piled into the library car. With great excitement they picked out books they wanted and tried to sit down, but only about half of them could find seats and the rest had to stand. It looked

123

exactly like a crowded train, with people reading books standing up. It was quite a funny sight.

The children were overjoyed. Totto-chan couldn't read too well yet, so she chose a book with a picture in it that looked most entertaining. When everyone had a book in hand and started turning the pages, the car suddenly became quiet. But not for long. The silence was soon broken by a jumble of voices. Some were reading passages aloud, some were asking others the meaning of characters they didn't know, and some wanted to swap books. Laughter filled the train. One child had just started on a book called *Singing Pictures* and was drawing a face while reading out the accompanying jingle in a loud singsong:

A circle and a spot; a circle and a spot;
Criss-crosses for the nose; another round and dot.
Three hairs, three hairs, three hairs—and wow!
Quick as a wink, there's a fat *hausfrau*.

The face had to be encircled on the word "wow," and the three semicircles drawn as you sang "Quick as a wink." If you made all the right strokes, the result was the face of a plump woman with an old-fashioned Japanese hairdo.

At Tomoe, where the children were allowed to

work on their subjects in any order they pleased, it would have been awkward if the children let themselves be disturbed by what others were doing. They were trained to concentrate no matter what was going on around them. So nobody paid any attention to the child singing aloud while drawing the *hausfrau*. One or two had joined in, but all the others were absorbed in their books.

Totto-chan's book seemed to be a folk tale. It was about a rich man's daughter who couldn't get a husband because she was always breaking wind. Finally her parents managed to find a husband for her, but she was so excited on her wedding night that she let out a much bigger one than ever before, and the wind blew her bridegroom out of bed, spun him around the bedroom seven and a half times, and knocked him unconscious. The picture that had looked so entertaining showed him flying through the room. Afterward, that book was always in great demand.

All the students of the school, packed into the train like sardines, devouring the books so eagerly in the morning sunlight that was pouring through the windows, must have presented a sight that gladdened the heart of the headmaster.

The children spent the whole of that day in the library car.

After that, when they couldn't be outdoors because of rain, and at many other times, the library became a favorite gathering place for them.

"I think I'd better have a bathroom built near the library," said the headmaster one day.

That was because the children would become so absorbed in their books that they were always holding out until the very last minute before making a dash for the toilet beyond the Assembly Hall with their bodies in strange contortions.

🌷 Tails

One afternoon, when school was over and Totto-chan was preparing to go home, Oe came running to her and whispered, "The headmaster's mad at somebody."

"Where?" asked Totto-chan.

She had never heard of the headmaster getting angry and was amazed. Oe was obviously amazed, too, the way he had come running in such a hurry to tell her.

"They're in the kitchen," said Oe, his good-natured eyes opened wide and his nostrils a little dilated.

"Come on!"

Totto-chan took Oe's hand and they both raced toward the headmaster's house. It adjoined the Assembly Hall, and the kitchen was right by the back entrance to the school grounds. The time Totto-chan fell into the cesspool she was taken through the kitchen to the bathroom to be scrubbed clean. And it was in the headmaster's kitchen that "something from the ocean and something from the hills" were made to be doled out at lunchtime.

As the two children tiptoed toward the kitchen, they heard the angry voice of the headmaster through the closed door.

"What made you say so thoughtlessly to Taka-hashi that he had a tail?"

It was their homeroom teacher who was being reprimanded.

"I didn't mean it seriously," they heard her reply. "I just happened to notice him at that moment, and he looked so cute."

"But can't you see the seriousness of what you said? What can I do to make you understand the care I take with regard to Takahashi?"

Totto-chan remembered what happened in class that morning. The homeroom teacher had been telling them about human beings originally having tails. The children had thought it great fun. Grown-ups would have probably called her talk an introduction to the theory of evolution. It appealed to the children greatly. And when the teacher told them everybody had the vestige of a tail called the coccyx, each child started wondering where his was, and soon the classroom was in an uproar. Finally the teacher had said, jokingly, "Maybe somebody here still has a tail! What about you, Takahashi?"

Takahashi had quickly stood up, shaking his head emphatically, and said in deadly earnest, "I haven't got one."

Totto-chan realized that was what the headmaster was talking about. His voice had now become more sad than angry.

"Did it occur to you to think how Takahashi might feel if he was asked if he had a tail?"

The children couldn't hear the teacher's reply. Totto-chan didn't understand why the headmaster was so angry about the tail. She would have loved being asked by the headmaster if she had a tail.

Of course, she had nothing wrong with her, so she wouldn't have minded such a question. But Takahashi had stopped growing, and he knew it. That was why the headmaster had thought up events for Sports Day in which Takahashi would do well. He had them swim in the pool without swimsuits so children like Takahashi would lose their self-consciousness. He did all he could to help children with physical handicaps, like Takahashi and Yasuaki-chan, lose any complexes they might have and the feeling they were inferior to other children. It was beyond the headmaster's comprehension how anyone could be so thoughtless as to ask Takahashi, just because he looked cute, whether he had a tail.

The headmaster happened to be visiting that class, standing in the back of the classroom, when she said it.

Totto-chan could hear the homeroom teacher crying. "It was terribly wrong of me," she sobbed. "What can I do to apologize to Takahashi?"

The headmaster said nothing. Totto-chan couldn't see him through the glass door, but she wanted so much to be with him. She didn't know what it was all about, but somehow she felt more than ever that he was their friend. Oe must have felt that way, too.

Totto-chan never forgot how the headmaster had reprimanded their homeroom teacher in his kitchen and not in the faculty room, where the other teachers were. It showed he was an educator in the very best sense of the word, although Totto-chan did not realize that at the time. The sound of his voice and his words remained in her heart forever.

It was almost spring, Totto-chan's second spring at Tomoe, and the beginning of a new school year.

Tender green leaves were sprouting on all the trees in the school grounds, and the flowers in the flower beds were busy blossoming. Crocuses, daffodils, and pansies popped out their heads in turn to say, "How do you do?" to the pupils of Tomoe, and the tulips lengthened their stalks as if stretching themselves. Cherry buds trembled in the soft breeze, all set and ready, waiting for the signal to burst into bloom.

The black popeyes, followed by the rest of the goldfish that lived in the small square concrete foot-rinsing basin by the swimming pool, shook themselves and started to swim about happily.

There was no need to say, "It's spring," for the season when everything looks shining and fresh and lively needed no announcement. Everyone knew it was spring!

It was exactly a year since the morning Totto-chan first arrived at Tomoe Gakuen with Mother. She was so surprised to find a gate growing out of the ground, and so excited to see classrooms in a train, that she jumped up and down, and so certain that Sosaku Kobayashi, the headmaster, was her friend. Now Totto-chan and her classmates rejoiced in their new status as second graders while in came the new first grade children looking all around curiously just as Totto-chan and her classmates had done.

It had been an eventful year for Totto-chan, and she had eagerly looked forward to every single morning of it. She still liked street musicians, but she had learned to like many, many more things around her. The little girl who had been expelled for being a nuisance had grown into a child worthy of Tomoe.

Some parents had misgivings about Tomoe's education. There were times when even Totto-chan's Mother and Daddy wondered if they had done the right thing. Among parents who regarded Mr. Kobayashi's educational system dubiously and judged it superficially, just by what they saw, were some who became so alarmed about leaving their children at his school that they arranged to transfer them elsewhere. But the children themselves did not want to leave Tomoe, and cried. Fortunately, no one was leaving in Totto-chan's class, but a boy one grade above had tears streaming down his cheeks as he vented his despair by pounding on the head-master's back with clenched fists, the scab from a grazed knee flapping all the while. The headmaster's eyes were red from crying, too. The lad was finally led away from the school by his mother and father. As he went, he kept on turning around and waving, time after time.

But there were not many sad occasions like that, and Totto-chan was now a second grader, with the expectation of more daily surprises and delight.

By this time Totto-chan's schoolbag was well acquainted with her back.

🌷 Swan Lake

Totto-chan was taken to Hibiya Hall to see the ballet *Swan Lake*. Daddy was playing the violin solo and a very fine troupe was performing. It was the first time she had ever been to a ballet. The queen of the swans wore a tiny sparkling crown on her head and leaped through the air effortlessly, like a real swan. Or so it seemed to Totto-chan. The prince fell in love with the swan queen and spurned all others. Finally, the two of them danced together so tenderly. The music, too, made a great impression on Totto-chan, and after she got home she couldn't stop thinking about it. Next day, when she woke up, she went straight down to the kitchen where Mother was, without even brushing her hair, and announced, "I don't want to be a spy any more, or a street musician, or a ticket seller. I'm going to be a ballerina and dance in *Swan Lake*!"

"Oh," said Mother. She didn't seem surprised.

It was the first time Totto-chan had ever seen a ballet, but she had heard a great deal from the headmaster about Isadora Duncan, an American lady who danced beautifully. Like Mr. Kobayashi, Isadora Duncan had been influenced by Dalcroze. If the headmaster she admired so much liked Isadora Duncan, that was enough for Totto-chan, and although she had never seen her dance, she felt as if she knew her. So to be a dancer didn't seem anything out of the ordinary to Totto-chan.

It so happened that a friend of Mr. Kobayashi's who came and taught eurythmics at Tomoe had a dance studio nearby. Mother arranged for Totto-chan to take lessons at his studio after school. Mother never told Totto-chan that she must do this or must do that, but when Totto-chan wanted to do something, she would agree, and, without asking all sorts of questions, she would go ahead and make the arrangements.

Totto-chan began taking lessons at the studio, longing for the day when she would be able to dance *Swan Lake*. But the teacher had his own special method. Besides the eurythmics they did at Tomoe, he would have the pupils amble about to piano or phonograph music, repeating to themselves some such phrase as "Shine upon the mountain!" from the prayer "Cleanse my soul; Oh, shine upon the mountain!" chanted by pilgrims as they climb Mount Fuji. Suddenly the teacher would exclaim, "Pose!" and the pupils would have to assume some pose they devised themselves and stand still. The teacher would pose, too, with some emotive cry like "Aach!" and assume a "looking up to heaven" pose or sometimes that of "a person in agony," crouching down and holding his head with both hands.

The image Totto-chan cherished in her mind, however, was that of a swan wearing a sparkling crown and a frilly white costume. It was not "Shine upon the mountain!" or "Aach!"

One day Totto-chan plucked up courage and went over to the teacher. Although he was a man, he had curly hair and bangs. Totto-chan stretched her arms out and fluttered them like the wings of a swan.

"Aren't we ever going to do anything like this?" she asked.

The teacher was a handsome man with large round eyes and an aquiline nose.

"We don't do that kind of dancing here," he said.

After that Totto-chan stopped going to his studio. True, she liked leaping about in bare feet, not wearing ballet shoes, and striking poses she thought up herself. But, after all, she did so want to wear one of those tiny, glittering crowns!

"*Swan Lake* is nice," said the teacher, "but I wish I could get you to like just dancing according to your fancy."

It wasn't until years later that Totto-chan found

out that his name was Baku Ishii and that he not only introduced free ballet to Japan but also gave the
name Jiyugaoka ("freedom hill") to the area. In addition to all that—he was fifty at the time—this man
tried to teach Totto-chan the joy of dancing freely.

The Farming Teacher

"This is your teacher today. He's going to show
you all sorts of things." With that the headmaster introduced a new teacher. Totto-chan took a good
look at him. In the first place, he wasn't dressed like
a teacher at all. He wore a short striped cotton work
jacket over his undershirt, and instead of a necktie,
he had a towel hanging around his neck. As for his
trousers, they were of indigo-dyed cotton with narrow legs, and were full of patches. Instead of shoes,
he wore workmen's thick two-toed rubber-soled
socks, while on his head was a rather dilapidated
straw hat.

The children were all assembled by the pond at
Kuhonbutsu Temple.

As she stared at the teacher, Totto-chan thought
she had seen him before. "Where?" she wondered.
His kindly face was sunburnt and full of wrinkles.
Even the slender pipe dangling from a black cord
around his waist that served as a belt looked
familiar. She suddenly remembered!

"Aren't you the farmer who works in the field by
the stream?" she asked him, delighted.

"That's right," said the "teacher," with a toothy
smile, wrinkling up his face. "You pass my place
ev'ry time you go fer yer walks to Kuhonbutsu!

That's my field. That one over there full o' mustard blossoms."

"Wow! So you're going to be our teacher today," cried the children excitedly.

"Naw!" said the man, waving his hand in front of his face. "I ain't no teacher! I'm just a farmer. Your headmaster just asked me to do it, that's all."

"Oh yes, he is. He's your farming teacher," said the headmaster, standing beside him. "He very kindly agreed to teach you how to plant a field. It's like having a baker teach you how to make bread. Now then," he said to the farmer, "tell the children what to do, and let's get started."

At an ordinary elementary school, anyone who taught the children anything would probably have to have teaching qualifications, but Mr. Kobayashi didn't worry about things like that. He thought it important for children to learn by actually seeing things done.

"Let's begin then," said the farming teacher.

The place where they were assembled was beside the Kuhonbutsu pond and it was a particularly quiet section—a pleasant place, where the pond was shaded by trees. The headmaster had already had part of a railroad car put there for storing the children's farming implements, such as spades and hoes. The half-car had a peaceful look, neatly placed as it was right in the middle of the plot they were going to cultivate.

The farming teacher told the children to get spades and hoes from the car and started them on weeding. He told them all about weeds: how hardy they were; how some grew faster than crops and hid the sun from them; how weeds were good hiding places for bad insects; and how weeds could be a nuisance by taking all the nourishment from the soil. He taught them one thing after another. And while he talked, his hands never stopped pulling out weeds. The children did the same. Then the teacher showed them how to hoe; how to make furrows; how to spread fertilizer; and everything else you had to do to grow things in a field, explaining as he demonstrated.

A little snake put its head out and very nearly bit the hand of Ta-chan, one of the older boys, but the farming teacher reassured him, "The snakes here ain't poisonous, and they won't hurt you if you don't hurt them."

Besides teaching the children how to plant a field, the farming teacher told them interesting things about insects, birds, and butterflies, about the weather, and about all sorts of other things. His strong gnarled hands seemed to attest that everything he told the children, he had found out himself through experience.

The children were dripping with perspiration when they had finally finished planting the field with the teacher's help. Except for a few furrows that were a bit uneven, it was an impeccable field, whichever way you looked at it.

From that day onward, the children held that farmer in high esteem, and whenever they saw him, even at a distance, they would cry, "There's our farming teacher!" Whenever he had any fertilizer left he would bring it over and spread it on the children's field, and their crops grew well. Every day someone would visit the field and report to the head-master and the other children on how it was doing.

The children learned to know the wonder and the joy of seeing the seeds they had planted themselves sprout. And whenever two or three of them were gathered together, talk would turn to the progress of their field.

Terrible things were beginning to happen in various parts of the world. But as the children discussed their tiny field, they were still enfolded in the very heart of peace.

🌷 Field Kitchen

One day, after school was over, Totto-chan went out the gate without speaking to anyone or even saying goodbye and hurried to Jiyugaoka Station, muttering to herself over and over, "Thunder canyon field kitchen, thunder canyon field kitchen. . . "

It was a difficult phrase for a little girl, but no worse than the name of that man in the comic *rakugo* tale whose name took so long to say he drowned in the well before his rescuers knew who he was. Totto-chan had to concentrate hard on the phrase, however, and if anyone nearby had suddenly started saying that famous long name that began, "Jugemu-Jugemu," she would have forgotten the phrase straight away. Even if she said, "Here we go," as she jumped over a puddle, she would be bound to get it muddled, so she could do nothing but keep on repeating it to herself. Thankfully, nobody tried to speak to her in the train and she tried not to discover anything interesting, so she managed to reach her station without even a single "What was that?" But as she was leaving the station, a man she recognized who worked there said, "Hello, back

136

already?" and she was on the point of replying but stopped herself, knowing it would mix her up, so she just waved to him and ran home.

The moment she reached the front door, she shouted to Mother at the top of her voice, "Thunder canyon field kitchen!" At first Mother wondered if it was a judo yell or a rallying cry of the Forty-seven Ronin. Then it clicked. Near Todoroki Station, three stops beyond Jiyugaoka, there was a famous beauty spot called Todoroki Keikoku, or Thunder Canyon. It was one of the most celebrated places of old Tokyo. It had a waterfall, a stream, and beautiful woods. As for field kitchen—that must mean the children were going to have a cookout there. What a difficult phrase to teach children, she marveled. But it proved how easily children learn once their interest is aroused.

Grateful to be released at last from the difficult phrase, Totto-chan gave Mother all the relevant details, one after the other. The children were to assemble at the school the following Friday morning. The things they had to bring were a soup bowl, a rice bowl, chopsticks, and one cup of uncooked rice. The headmaster said it became two bowlfuls when cooked, she remembered to add. They were going to make pork soup, too, so she needed some pork and vegetables. And they could bring something for an afternoon snack if they wanted.

The next few days Totto-chan stuck close to Mother in the kitchen and carefully observed how she used a knife, how she held a pot, and how she served the rice. It was nice watching her work in the kitchen, but what Totto-chan liked most was the way Mother would say, "Ooh, that's hot!" and quickly put her thumb and index finger to her earlobe whenever she picked up something hot like a lid.

"That's because earlobes are cold," Mother explained.

Her gesture impressed Totto-chan as being very grown-up and evidence of kitchen expertise. She said to herself, "When we thunder-canyon-field-kitchen, I'm going to do that, too!"

Friday finally arrived. When they had reached Thunder Canyon after leaving the train, the headmaster surveyed the children gathered in the woods. Their dear little faces glowed in the sunlight as it filtered through the tall trees. With their knapsacks

bulging, the children waited to hear what the head-master had to say, while beyond them the famous waterfall fell in booming torrents, making a beautiful rhythm.

"Now then," said the headmaster, "first of all, let's divide into groups and make stoves with the bricks the teachers have brought. Then some of you can wash the rice in the stream and put it on to cook. After that, we'll start making the pork soup. Now then, shall we get started?"

The children divided themselves into groups by playing "stone, paper, scissors." Since there were only about fifty of them, it wasn't long before they had six groups. Holes were dug and surrounded with piled-up bricks. Then they laid thin iron bars across to support the soup and rice pots. While that was going on, some gathered firewood in the forest, and others went off to wash the rice in the stream. The children themselves allotted their various tasks. Totto-chan offered to cut up the vegetables and take charge of the pork soup. A boy two years senior to Totto-chan was also assigned to chopping vegetables, but he cut them into pieces that were either too big or too small and made a mess of the job. He labored manfully with the task, however, his nose glistening with perspiration. Totto-chan followed Mother's example and skillfully cut up the egg-plants, potatoes, onions, burdock roots, and so forth, that the children had brought, in just the right bite-sized pieces. She even took it upon herself to make some pickles by slicing eggplant and cucumber very thin and rubbing the slices with salt. She gave advice, too, to some of the older children who were having trouble with their chores. Totto-chan really felt as if she had already become a mother! Everyone was impressed with her pickles.

"Oh, I just thought I'd try and see if I could make some," she declared modestly.

When it came to flavoring the pork broth, everyone was asked for an opinion. From the various groups came startled cries of, "Wow!" "Gee!" and a great deal of laughter. The birds in the forest twittered, too, joining in the general uproar. In the meantime, tempting aromas rose from every pot. Until then, hardly any of the children had ever watched something cooking or had to regulate the heat. They had merely eaten what was put before them on the table. The joy of cooking something themselves, with its attendant traumas—and seeing the various changes the ingredients have to undergo—was a whole new experience to them.

Eventually, the work at each group's makeshift stove was completed. The headmaster had the children make a space on the grass where they could all sit in a circle. One soup pot and one rice pot were placed in front of each group. But Totto-chan refused to have her group's soup pot taken away until she had first performed the action she had set her heart upon. Taking off the hot lid, she declared rather self-consciously, "Ooh, that's hot!" and put the fingers of both hands to her earlobes. Only then did she say, "You can take it now," and the pot was duly carried over to where the children were sitting, wondering what on earth was going on. No one seemed at all impressed. But Totto-chan was satisfied all the same.

Everyone's attention was fixed on the bowls of rice in front of them and the contents of the steaming soup bowls. The children were hungry. But first and foremost, it was a meal they had made themselves!

After the children had sung, "Chew, chew, chew it well, Everything you eat," and had said, "I gratefully partake," all became quiet in the woods. There was no sound but that of the waterfall.

🌷 "You're Really a Good Girl"

"You're really a good girl, you know."

That's what the headmaster used to say every time he saw Totto-chan. And every time he said it, Totto-chan would smile, give a little skip, and say, "Yes, I am a good girl." And she believed it.

Totto-chan was, indeed, a good girl in many ways. She was kind to everyone—particularly her physically handicapped friends. She would defend them, and, if children from other schools said cruel things, she would fight the tormentors, even if it ended with her crying. She would do everything to care for any injured animals she found. But at the same time her teachers were continually astonished at the amount of trouble she always got into as she tried to satisfy her curiosity whenever she discovered anything unusual.

She would do things like making her pigtails stick out behind under each arm while marching to morning assembly. Once, when it was her turn to sweep the classroom, she opened a trapdoor her sharp eyes had noticed in the floor and put all the sweepings down the hole. It had originally been for inspecting the machinery when it was a real train. But she couldn't get the trapdoor closed again, and caused everyone a lot of trouble. And then there was the time someone told her how meat was hung up on hooks, so she went and hung by one arm from the highest exercise bar. She hung there for ages, and when a teacher saw her and asked what she was doing, she shouted, "I'm a piece of meat today!" and just then lost her hold and fell down so hard it knocked all the wind out of her lungs and she couldn't speak all day. Then, of course, there was that time when she jumped into the cesspool.

She was always doing things like that and hurting herself, but the headmaster never sent for Mother and Daddy. It was the same with the other children. Matters were always settled between the headmaster and the child concerned. Just as he had listened to Totto-chan for four hours the day she first arrived at the school, he always listened to what a child had to say about an incident caused. He even listened to their excuses. And if the child had done something really bad and eventually recognized it was wrong, the headmaster would say, "Now apologize."

In Totto-chan's case, complaints and fears voiced by children's parents and other teachers undoubtedly reached the ears of the headmaster. That's why, whenever he had a chance, he would say to Totto-chan, "You're really a good girl, you know." A grown-up, hearing him say it, would have realized the significance of the way he emphasized the word "really."

What the headmaster must have wanted to make Totto-chan understand was something like this: "Some people may think you're not a good girl in many respects, but your real character is not bad. It has a great deal that is good about it, and I am well aware of that." Alas, it was many, many years before Totto-chan realized what he really meant. Still, while she may not have grasped his true meaning at the time, the headmaster certainly instilled, deep in her, a confidence in herself as "a good girl." His words echoed in her heart even when she was engaged in some escapade. And many times she said to herself, "Good heavens!" as she reflected on something she had done.

Mr. Kobayashi kept on repeating, the entire time she was at Tomoe, those important words that probably determined the course of her whole life:

"Totto-chan, you're really a good girl, you know."

His Bride

Totto-chan was very sad.

She was in third grade now and she liked Tai-chan a lot. He was clever and good at physics. He studied English, and it was he who taught her the English word for fox.

"Totto-chan," he had said, "do you know what the English word for *kitsune* is? It's 'fox.'"

"Fox."

Totto-chan had luxuriated in the sound of that word all day long. After that, the first thing she always did when she got to the classroom-in-the-train was to sharpen all the pencils in Tai-chan's pencil box as beautifully as she could with her penknife. She didn't bother about her own, which she just hacked at with her teeth.

In spite of all that, Tai-chan had spoken roughly to her. It happened during lunch break. Totto-chan was sauntering along behind the Assembly Hall in the region of that notorious cesspool.

"Totto-chan!"

Tai-chan's voice sounded cross, and she stopped, startled. Pausing for breath, Tai-chan said, "When I grow up, I'm not going to marry you, no matter how much you ask me to." So saying, he walked off, his eyes on the ground.

Totto-chan stood dazed, watching until he and his large head disappeared from view. That head full of brains that she admired so much. That head that looked so much bigger than his body the children used to call him "The Improper Fraction."

Totto-chan put her hands in her pockets and thought. She could not remember doing anything to annoy him. In desperation she talked it over with her classmate Miyo-chan. After listening to Totto-chan, Miyo-chan said, maturely, "Why, of course! It's because you threw Tai-chan out of the ring today at sumo wrestling. It's not surprising he flew out of

144

the ring the way he did because his head's so heavy. But he's still bound to be mad at you."

Totto-chan regretted it with all her heart. Yes, that was it. What on earth made her beat the boy she liked so much she sharpened his pencils every day? But it was too late. She could never be his bride now.

"I'm going to go on sharpening his pencils all the same," Totto-chan decided. "After all, I love him."

⚘ "Shabby Old School"

There was a jingle—a sort of singsong refrain—that was popular among elementary school children. They did it a lot at her previous school. As the children went home after school, they would go out the gate looking back over their shoulders at their school and chant:

> Akamatsu School's a shabby old school;
> Inside though, it's a splendid school!

When children from some other school happened to pass by, these pupils would point their fingers at Akamatsu School and chant:

> Akamatsu School's a splendid school;
> Inside though, it's a shabby old school!

And they would end by making a rude noise.

Whether a school was shabby or splendid in the first line depended on whether the building was old or new. The important part of the chant was the second line. The part that said what the school was like inside. So it didn't really matter if the first line said your school was shabby on the outside. It was what it was like inside that mattered. The jingle was always chanted by at least five or six children together.

One afternoon after school the Tomoe pupils were playing as usual. They could do anything they liked until the final bell, when they had to leave the school grounds. The headmaster thought it was important for children to have time when they were free to do whatever they liked, so this period after classes were over was longer than at other elementary schools. That day some were playing ball, some had made themselves all dirty playing on the iron bars or in the sandbox, some were tending the flower beds, some of the older girls were just sitting on the steps chatting, and some were climbing trees. They were all doing just what they wanted. Among them were a few, like Tai-chan, who had stayed behind in the classroom to continue a physics experiment and were boiling flasks and doing experiments in test tubes. There were children in the library reading, and Amadera, who liked animals, was scrutinizing a stray cat he had found, turning it on its back and examining inside its ears. They were all enjoying themselves in their own ways.

Suddenly, a loud chant was heard outside the school:

Tomoe School is a shabby old school;
Inside, too, it's a shabby old school!

"That's terrible," thought Totto-chan. She happened to be right by the gate. Well, it wasn't really a gate, as it had leaves growing out of the posts. But at any rate, she heard them very clearly. It was too much. Imagine calling their school shabby both inside and out! She was indignant. The others were indignant, too, and came running toward the gate. "Shabby old school!" reiterated the boys from the other school, as they ran off making rude noises.

Totto-chan was so infuriated she ran after the boys. All by herself. But they were very fast, running down a side street and disappearing as quick as a wink. Totto-chan walked back to school disconsolately. As she walked, she sang:

Tomoe School is a wonderful school;

A few steps along, she added:

Inside and out, it's a wonderful school!

She liked it, and it made her feel better. So when she got back, she pretended she was from another school and shouted through the hedge in a loud voice, so that everybody could hear:

Tomoe School is a wonderful school;
Inside and out, it's a wonderful school!

The children playing in the grounds at first couldn't imagine who it was. When they realized it was Totto-chan, they went out to the road and joined in. Finally they all linked arms and marched along the roads surrounding the school chanting together. It was their hearts that were in unison even more than their voices, although they didn't realize that then. The more they went around the school, the more they entered into the spirit of it.

Tomoe School is a wonderful school;
Inside and out, it's a wonderful school!

The children little knew, of course, what happiness their chant was giving the headmaster, as he sat listening in his office.

It must be the same for any educator, but for those in particular who truly think about the children, running a school must be a daily series of agonies. It must have been even more so at a school like Tomoe, where everything was so unusual. The school could not escape criticism from people used to a more conventional system of education.

In such circumstances, that song of the children was the nicest gift they could possibly have given the headmaster.

Tomoe School is a wonderful school;
Inside and out, it's a wonderful school!

That day the final bell rang later than usual.

🌷 The Hair Ribbon

One day at lunch break, after the children had finished eating, Totto-chan was skipping across the Assembly Hall when she met the headmaster. It is perhaps odd to say she met the headmaster when he had been with them all through lunch, but she met him because he was coming from the opposite direction.

"Oh, there you are," said the headmaster. "I've been wanting to ask you something."

"What is it?" asked Totto-chan, delighted to think she could give the headmaster some information.

"Where did you get that ribbon?" he asked, looking at the bow she had in her hair.

The expression on Totto-chan's face when she

148

heard that couldn't have been a happier one. She had been wearing the bow since the day before. It was something she had found herself. She went up closer so the headmaster could see the ribbon better.

"It was on my aunt's old school uniform," she said proudly. "I noticed it when she was putting it in a drawer and she gave it to me. Auntie said I was very observant."

"I see," said the headmaster, deep in thought.

Totto-chan was very proud of the ribbon. She told him how she had gone to see her aunt and was lucky to find her aunt airing some clothes. Among them was the old-fashioned, long, purple pleated skirt she had worn when she was a schoolgirl. As her aunt was putting it away, Totto-chan noticed something pretty on it.

"What's that?"

At Totto-chan's question, her aunt paused. The something pretty turned out to be this ribbon that was attached to the waistband at the back.

"It was supposed to make you look pretty from the back," said Auntie. "In those days everyone wanted to put a piece of handmade lace there or a wide ribbon tied in a big bow."

She noticed how longingly Totto-chan gazed at the bow as she listened, stroking it and feeling it, and said, "I'll give it to you. I shan't be wearing it again."

She took some scissors and cut the thread attaching it to the skirt and gave it to Totto-chan. That was how she got it. It really was a beautiful ribbon. It was wide and of very good silk, and had roses and all sorts of designs woven into it. Wide and stiff when it was tied, it made a bow as big as Totto-chan's head. Auntie said the fabric was imported.

While she was speaking, Totto-chan jiggled her head occasionally so the headmaster could hear the rustling sound the ribbon made. When he had heard her story, the headmaster looked a little distressed.

"So that's it," he said. "Yesterday Miyo-chan said she wanted a ribbon just like yours, so I went to all the ribbon shops in Jiyugaoka, but they didn't have anything like it. So that's it. It's imported, is it?"

His face was more like that of a troubled father importuned by his daughter than of a headmaster.

"Totto-chan, I'd be truly grateful if you'd stop wearing that ribbon to school. You see, Miyo-chan keeps pestering me about it. Would you mind very much?"

Totto-chan thought it over, her arms folded. Then she answered quickly, "All right. I won't wear it here any more."

"Thank you," said the headmaster.

Totto-chan was rather sorry, but the headmaster was in trouble, so she had agreed. Another reason was that the thought of a grown-up man—her beloved headmaster—searching high and low in all the ribbon shops, made her feel sorry for him. That was the way it was at Tomoe. Without realizing it, everyone got in the habit of understanding one another's problems and trying to help, irrespective of age. It became the natural thing to do.

The following morning, when Mother went into Totto-chan's room to clean up after Totto-chan had left for school, she found the ribbon tied around the neck of Totto-chan's favorite teddy bear. She wondered why Totto-chan had suddenly given up wearing the ribbon she had been so thrilled about. Mother thought the gray teddy bear looked slightly embarrassed about being dressed so gaily all of a sudden.

꧁ Visiting the Wounded

For the first time in her life Totto-chan visited a hospital for wounded soldiers. She went with about thirty elementary school children from various schools, children she didn't know. It was part of a scheme recently organized nationally for groups of elementary school children. Each school would normally send two or three children, but small schools like Tomoe only sent one, and the group would be in the charge of a teacher from one of the schools. Totto-chan was representing Tomoe.

The teacher in charge was a thin woman who wore glasses. She led the children into a ward where there were about fifteen soldiers in white pajamas, some in bed and others walking about. Totto-chan had worried about what wounded soldiers would look like, but they all smiled and waved their hands and seemed cheerful so she was relieved, although some had bandages on their heads.

The teacher assembled the children in the middle of the ward and addressed the soldiers.

"We've come to visit you," she said, and the children all bowed. The teacher went on, "Since today is the fifth of May—Boy's Day—we're going to sing 'Carp Streamers.' "

She raised her arms, like a conductor, said to the children, "Now, ready? Three, four," and began to beat time. The children didn't know each other but they all began singing wholeheartedly:

Over the sea of rooftops,
Over the sea of clouds . . .

Totto-chan didn't know the song. They didn't
teach that sort of song at Tomoe. She sat on the
edge of the bed of a man with a kind face who was
sitting up, and just listened to them singing, feeling
rather awkward. When that song was over, the
teacher announced very clearly, "Now we shall sing
'The Doll Festival.'" They sang it beautifully. All except Totto-chan.

Come let us light the lanterns,
Light them one by one . . .

There was nothing Totto-chan could do but remain silent.

When they had all finished singing, the men clapped. The teacher smiled and said, "Now then, what
about 'The Pony and the Mare'? All together. Three,
four," and started beating time again.

Totto-chan didn't know that one either. When
the children had finished singing it, the soldier in the
bed Totto-chan was sitting on patted her head and
said, "You didn't sing."

Totto-chan felt very apologetic. She had come to
visit the soldiers and she couldn't even sing them a
single song. So she got up, and, standing a little away
from the bed, said bravely, "All right. Now I'll sing
one I know."

Something was about to happen that wasn't
according to plan.

"What are you going to sing?" asked the teacher.
But Totto-chan had already taken a deep breath and
was starting to sing, so she decided to wait.

Since she was representing Tomoe, Totto-chan thought she had better sing Tomoe's best-known song. After taking that deep breath, she began:

> Chew, chew, chew it well,
> Everything you eat . . .

Some of the children laughed. Others asked their neighbors, "What's the song? What's the song?" The teacher started to beat time, but not knowing quite what to do, was left with arms in midair. Totto-chan was embarrassed, but she sang for all she was worth:

> Chew it and chew it and chew it and chew it,
> Your rice and fish and meat!

When she finished singing, Totto-chan bowed. When she raised her head, she was astonished to see tears streaming down the face of the soldier. She thought she must have done something bad. And then the soldier, who looked a little older than Daddy, patted her head again, and said, "Thank you! Thank you!"

He went on patting her head, and he couldn't stop crying. Then the teacher said brightly, as if to try and cheer him up, "Now I think it's time to read out the compositions we've written for the soldiers."

The children took turns reading their compositions aloud. Totto-chan looked at her soldier. His nose and eyes were red, but he smiled. Totto-chan smiled back. And she thought to herself, "I'm so glad the soldier smiled!"

What had brought tears to that soldier's eyes, only the soldier knew. Maybe he had a little girl like Totto-chan. Or maybe he was simply touched by the sweet way she sang that song as best she could. Or maybe because of his experience at the war front, he knew how near they all were to starvation, and the thought of this little girl singing "Chew it well" when there might soon be nothing left to chew may have filled him with sadness. The soldier may also have realized what terrible events would soon engulf these very children.

The children, reading their compositions, may not have sensed it then, but the Pacific War was already well underway.

🌷 Health Bark

Showing her train pass on the cord around her neck to the man at the gate—whom she now knew quite well—Totto-chan walked out of the station at Jiyugaoka.

Something very interesting was going on. A young man was sitting cross-legged on a mat behind an enormous pile of what looked like pieces of tree bark. Five or six people stood around looking down at him. Totto-chan decided to join them, since the man was saying, "Now watch me carefully, watch me carefully." When the man saw Totto-chan stop, he said, "The most important thing for you is health. When you get up in the morning and want to know whether you are well or not, this piece of bark will tell you. Every morning all you have to do is chew a bit of this bark. If it tastes bitter, it proves you are not well. If it doesn't taste bitter, you know you're all right. You're not ill. This bark that tells you whether you're ill or not only costs twenty sen! Will that gentleman over there care to try a piece?"

He handed the bark to a rather thin man, who timidly bit it with his front teeth. The man tilted his head slightly and considered it.

"It does seem . . . a tiny bit . . . uh . . . bitter."

The young man leaped up, exclaiming, "Sir, you must be suffering from some disease. You'll have to be careful. But don't worry, it's not very serious yet. You said it just seemed a little bitter. Now what about the lady over there. Would you mind chewing this, please?" A woman with a shopping basket took a larger piece of bark and chewed it vigorously. She announced cheerfully, "Why, that wasn't bitter at all!"

"Congratulations, madam," said the man. "You must be very healthy, indeed." Then he said, raising his voice, "Only twenty sen! Twenty sen! That's all it costs to find out every morning whether you are healthy or not. A real bargain!"

Totto-chan wanted to try a bite of the grayish bark, too, but was too shy to ask. Instead, she asked, "Will you still be here when school's over?"

"Sure," said the man, glancing at the young schoolchild.

Totto-chan ran off, her bag flapping against her back. She didn't want to be late since there was something she had to do before school began. She had to ask the children something the moment she got to her classroom.

"Can anybody lend me twenty sen?"

But nobody had twenty sen. One of those long packets of caramels only cost ten sen, so it wasn't very much money, really, but nobody had it.

"Shall I ask my parents?" asked Miyo-chan.

At times like these it was very convenient that

155

Miyo-chan happened to be the daughter of the headmaster. Miyo-chan's house adjoined the Assembly Hall, so it was just as if her mother lived at the school.

"Daddy says he'll lend it to you," she told Totto-chan at lunchtime, "but he wants to know what it's for."

Totto-chan made her way to the office.

"So you want twenty sen," he said, taking off his glasses. "What do you want it for?"

"I want to buy a piece of bark that tells you whether you're sick or whether you're well," she replied quickly. The headmaster's curiosity was aroused.

"Where are they selling them?"

"In front of the station," she replied, in a great hurry.

"All right," said the headmaster. "Buy one if you want. But let me have a bite, won't you?"

He took a purse out of his jacket pocket and placed twenty sen in Totto-chan's palm.

"Oh, thank you so much!" said Totto-chan. "I'll get the money from Mother and pay you back. She always gives me money for books. If I want to buy anything else I have to ask first, but health bark is something everybody needs so I'm sure she won't mind."

When school was over, Totto-chan hurried to the station, clutching her twenty sen. The man was still there, extolling his product in a loud patter. When he saw the twenty sen in Totto-chan's hand, he broke into a broad grin.

"Good girl! Your mother and father'll be pleased."

"So will Rocky," said Totto-chan.

"Who's Rocky?" asked the man, as he picked out a piece of bark for Totto-chan.

"He's our dog. He's a German shepherd."

The man stopped and thought for a minute, then said, "A dog . . . well, I suppose it'll work with a dog, too. After all, if it's bitter he won't like it and that'll mean he's ill."

The man picked out a piece of bark about one inch wide and six inches long.

"Here you are. Bite some every morning and if it's bitter, you're sick. If not, you're as fit as a fiddle!"

Totto-chan went home carefully carrying the

157

precious bark wrapped in newspaper. The first thing she did when she got there was to take a small bite. It was dry and rough, but not bitter. In fact, it didn't taste of anything at all.

"Hooray! I'm healthy!"

"Of course you are," said Mother, smiling. "What on earth's the matter?"

Totto-chan explained. Mother tried biting a piece of the bark, too.

"It's not bitter."

"Then you're healthy, too, Mother!"

Then Totto-chan went over to Rocky and held the bark to his mouth. First Rocky sniffed it. Then he licked it.

"You've got to *bite* it," said Totto-chan. "Then you'll know whether you're sick or not."

But Rocky made no attempt to bite it. He just scratched the back of his ear with his paw. Totto-chan held the tree bark closer to his mouth.

"Come on, bite it! It would be terrible if you weren't well."

Rocky reluctantly bit a tiny piece off the edge. Then he sniffed it again, but he didn't look as if he particularly disliked it. He just let out a big yawn.

"Hooray! Rocky's healthy, too!"

Next morning, Mother gave Totto-chan twenty sen. She went straight to the headmaster's office and thrust out the tree bark.

For a moment the headmaster looked at it as if to say, "What's this?" Then he saw the twenty sen Totto-chan had brought him, clutched carefully in her hand, and remembered.

"Bite it," said Totto-chan. "If it's bitter, it means you're ill."

158

The headmaster bit some. Then he turned the bark over and studied it carefully.

"Does it taste bitter?" asked Totto-chan, concerned, looking at the headmaster's face.

"It hasn't any taste at all."

As he returned the bark to Totto-chan, he said, "I'm fine. Thank you."

"Hooray! The headmaster's healthy! I'm so glad."

That day Totto-chan got everybody in the school to bite a piece of bark. Not a single child found it bitter, which meant they were all healthy. Totto-chan was very glad.

The children all went and told the headmaster they were healthy, and to each child the headmaster replied, "That's good."

The headmaster must have known all along. He was born and bred in the heart of the country in Gumma Prefecture, beside a river from which you could see Mount Haruna. He must have known that the bark would not taste bitter, no matter who chewed it.

But the headmaster thought it was nice for Totto-chan to be so glad to find that everyone was healthy. He was happy that Totto-chan had been brought up to be the kind of person who would have been worried and concerned about anyone who might have said the bark tasted bitter.

Totto-chan even tried pushing the tree bark into the mouth of a stray dog walking near the school. She almost got bitten, but that didn't daunt her.

"You'll know whether you're sick or not," she shouted at the dog. "Come on, bite it! 'Cause if you're healthy, then that's fine."

She succeeded in getting that dog she didn't know

to bite a piece. Skipping around the dog she cried, "Hooray! You're healthy, too!"

The dog bowed its head, as if thanking her, and ran off.

Just as the headmaster guessed, the bark-seller never showed up in Jiyugaoka again.

Every morning, before she left for school, Totto-chan took the precious piece of bark from her drawer—it now looked as if an energetic beaver had been at it—and chewed some of it, calling out as she left the house, "I'm healthy!"

And, thankfully, Totto-chan was in fact healthy.

🌷 The English-speaking Child

A new pupil arrived at Tomoe. He was tall for an elementary school boy, and broad. Totto-chan thought he looked more like a seventh grader. His clothes were different, too, more like grown-up ones.

That morning in the school grounds the head-master introduced the new student.

"This is Miyazaki. He was born and brought up in America, so he doesn't speak Japanese very well. That's why he has come to Tomoe, where he will be able to make friends more easily and take his time over his studies. He's one of you now. What grade shall we put him in? What about fifth grade, with Ta-chan and the others?"

"That's fine," said Ta-chan—who was good at drawing—in a big-brotherly voice.

The headmaster smiled and went on, "I said he wasn't very good at Japanese, but he's very good at English. Get him to teach you some. He's not used to life in Japan, though, so you'll help him, won't

160

you? And ask him about life in America. He'll be able to tell you all sorts of interesting things. Well, then, I'll leave him with you."

Miyazaki bowed to his classmates, who were all much smaller than he was. And all the children, not only the children in Ta-chan's class, bowed back.

At lunchtime Miyazaki went over to the head-master's house, and all the others followed him. Then what did he do but start to walk into the house with his shoes on! All the children shouted at him, "You've got to take off your shoes!"

Miyazaki seemed startled. "Oh, excuse me," he said, taking them off.

The children began telling him what to do, all talking at once.

"You have to take your shoes off for rooms with tatami-matted floors and for the Assembly Hall. You can keep them on in the classrooms and in the library."

"When you go to Kuhonbutsu Temple you can keep them on in the courtyard but you have to take them off in the temple."

It was fun learning about the differences between living in Japan and living abroad.

Next day Miyazaki brought a big English picture book to school. They all clustered around him at lunchtime to look at the book. They were amazed. They had never seen such a beautiful picture book before. The picture books they knew were only printed in bright reds, greens, and yellows, but this one had pale flesh-colored pinks. As for the blues, they were lovely shades, mixed with white and gray—colors that didn't exist in crayons. There were lots of colors besides the standard twenty-four in a box of crayons, colors that were not even in Ta-chan's special box of forty-eight. Everyone was impressed. As for the pictures, the first one was of a dog pulling a baby by its diaper. What impressed them was that the baby didn't look as if it was painted but had soft pink skin just like a real baby. They had never seen a picture book that was so big and printed on such lovely, thick, shiny paper. In her usual sociable way, Totto-chan got as close to Miyazaki and the picture book as she could.

Miyazaki read the English text to them. The English language sounded so smooth that they listened enraptured. Then Miyazaki began to grapple with Japanese.

Miyazaki certainly had brought something new and different to the school.

"*Akachan* is baby," he began.

They all repeated it after him. "*Akachan* is baby."

"*UtsuKUshi* is beautiful," Miyazaki said next, stressing the "*ku.*"

"*UtsukuSHII* is beautiful," repeated the others.

Miyazaki then realized his Japanese pronunciation had been wrong. "It's *utsukuSHII*, is it? Right?"

Miyazaki and the other children soon became good friends. Every day he brought various books to Tomoe and read them to the others at lunchtime.

It was just as if Miyazaki was their English tutor. At the same time Miyazaki's Japanese quickly improved. And he stopped making blunders like sitting in the *tokonoma*, the alcove reserved for hanging-scrolls and ornaments.

Totto-chan and her friends learned lots of things about America. Japan and America were becoming friends at Tomoe. But outside Tomoe, America had become an enemy, and since English had become an enemy language, it was dropped from the curriculum of all the schools.

"Americans are devils," the government announced. But at Tomoe the children kept chanting in chorus, "*Utsukushii* is beautiful." And the breezes that blew across Tomoe were soft and warm, and the children themselves were beautiful.

🪷 Amateur Drama

"We're going to put on a play!"

It was the first play in Tomoe's history. The custom of someone giving a talk at lunchtime was still going on, but imagine performing a play on the little stage with the grand piano the headmaster always played for eurythmics and inviting an audience. None of the children had even seen a play, not even Totto-chan. Apart from *Swan Lake*, she had never once been to the theater. Nevertheless, they all discussed what sort of program they should put on for their end-of-year performance.

Totto-chan's class decided to do *Kanjincho* ("The Fund-Raising Charter"). This famous old Kabuki play was not exactly what you would expect to see at Tomoe, but it was in one of their textbooks and Mr. Maruyama would coach them. They decided Aiko Saisho would make a good Benkei, the strong man, since she was big and tall, and Amadera, who could look stern and had a loud voice, should play Togashi, the commander. After talking it over, they all came to the conclusion that Totto-chan should be the noble Yoshitsune, who, in the play, is disguis-

163

ed as a porter. All the others would be strolling monks.

Before they could begin rehearsing, the children had to learn their lines. It was nice for Totto-chan and the monks, for they had nothing to say. All that the monks were required to do was stand silently throughout, while Totto-chan, as Yoshitsune, had to remain kneeling, with her face hidden by a large straw hat. Benkei, in reality Yoshitsune's servant, beats and upbraids his master in a clever attempt to get the party past the Ataka Checkpoint by posing as a band of monks collecting funds to restore a temple. Aiko Saisho, playing Benkei, had a tremendous part. Besides all the verbal thrust and parry with Togashi, the checkpoint commander, there was the exciting bit where Benkei has to pretend to read out the Fund-Raising Charter when ordered by the commander to do so. The scroll he "reads" from is blank, and he brilliantly extemporizes an appeal for funds in pompous ecclesiastical language: "Firstly, for the purpose of the restoration of the temple known as Todaiji . . ."

Aiko Saisho practiced her "Firstly" speech every day.

The role of Togashi, too, had lots of dialogue, as he tries to refute Benkei's arguments, and Amadera struggled to memorize it.

Finally rehearsal time came. Togashi and Benkei faced each other, with the monks lined up behind Benkei, and Totto-chan, as Yoshitsune, kneeling, huddled over, in front. But Totto-chan didn't understand what it was all about. So when Benkei had to knock Yoshitsune down with his staff and strike him, Totto-chan reacted violently. She kicked

Aiko Saisho in the legs and scratched her. Aiko cried and the monks giggled.

Yoshitsune was supposed to remain still, looking cowed, no matter how much Benkei beat and hit him. The idea is that while Togashi suspects the truth, he is so impressed by Benkei's ruse and the pain it must cost him to ill-treat his noble master, that he lets them through the checkpoint.

To have Yoshitsune resisting would ruin the whole plot. Mr. Maruyama tried to explain this to Totto-chan. But Totto-chan was adamant. She insisted that if Aiko Saisho hit her she would hit back. So they made no progress.

No matter how many times they tried the scene, Totto-chan always put up a fight.

"I'm terribly sorry," said Mr. Maruyama to Totto-chan finally, "but I think we had better ask Tai-chan to play the part of Yoshitsune."

Totto-chan was relieved. She didn't like being the only one who got knocked about.

"Totto-chan, will you please be a monk?" asked Mr. Maruyama. So Totto-chan stood with the other monks, but right at the back.

Mr. Maruyama and the children thought everything would be fine now, but they were wrong. He shouldn't have let Totto-chan have a monk's long staff. Totto-chan got bored with standing still so she started poking the feet of the monk next to her with the staff, and tickling the monk in front under his armpits. She even pretended to conduct with it, which was not only dangerous for those nearby but also ruined the scene between Benkei and Togashi.

So eventually she was deprived of her role as a monk, too.

Tai-chan as Yoshitsune, gritted his teeth manfully as he was knocked over and beaten, and the audience must surely have felt sorry for him. Rehearsals progressed smoothly without Totto-chan.

Left by herself, Totto-chan went out into the school grounds. She took off her shoes and started to improvise a Totto-chan ballet. It was lovely dancing according to her own fancy. Sometimes she was a swan, sometimes the wind, sometimes a grotesque person, sometimes a tree. All alone in the deserted playground she danced and danced.

Deep in her heart, however, there was a tiny feeling that she would like to be playing Yoshitsune. But had they allowed her to, she would surely have hit and scratched Aiko Saisho.

Thus it was that Totto-chan was not able to take part in the first and last amateur drama at Tomoe.

🌷 Chalk

Tomoe children never scrawled on other people's walls or on the road. That was because they had ample opportunity for doing it at school.

During music periods in the Assembly Hall, the headmaster would give each child a piece of white chalk. They could lie or sit anywhere they liked on the floor and wait, chalk in hand. When they were all ready, the headmaster started playing the piano. As he did so, they would write the rhythms, in musical notation, on the floor. It was lovely writing in chalk on the shiny light brown wood. There were only about ten pupils in Totto-chan's class, so when they were spread around the large Assembly Hall, they had plenty of floor on which to write their notes as large as they wanted without encroaching on anyone else's space. They didn't need lines for their notation, since they just wrote down the rhythm. At Tomoe musical notes had special names the children devised themselves after talking it over with the headmaster. Here they are:

was called a skip, because it was a good rhythm to skip and jump to.

was called a flag, because it looked like one.

was called a flag-flag.

was called a double-flag.

was called a black.

was called a white.

was called a white-with-a-mole, or a white 'n' dot.

was called a circle.

This way they learned to know the notes well and it was fun. It was a class they loved.

Writing on the floor with chalk was the headmaster's idea. Paper wasn't big enough and there weren't enough blackboards to go around. He thought the Assembly Hall floor would make a nice big blackboard on which the children could note the rhythm with ease no matter how fast the music was, and writing as large as they liked. Above all, they could enjoy the music. And if there was time afterward, they could draw airplanes and dolls and anything they wanted. Sometimes the children would join up their drawings just for fun and the whole floor would become one enormous picture.

At intervals during the music class, the headmaster would come over and inspect each child's rhythms. He would comment, "That's good," or "It wasn't a flag-flag there, it was a skip."

After he had approved or corrected their notation, he played the music over again so they could check what they had done and familiarize themselves with the rhythms. No matter how busy he was, the headmaster never let anyone else take these classes for him. And as far as the children were concerned, it wouldn't have been any fun at all without Mr. Kobayashi.

Cleaning up after writing rhythms was quite a job. First you had to wipe the floor with a blackboard eraser, and then everyone joined forces to make the floor spick and span again with mops and rags. It was an enormous task.

In this way Tomoe children learned what trouble cleaning off graffiti could be, so they never scribbled anywhere except on the floor of the Assembly Hall. Moreover, this class took place about twice a week, so the children had their fill of scribbling.

The children at Tomoe became real experts on chalk—which kind was best, how to hold it, how to manipulate it for the best results, how not to break it. Every one of them was a chalk connoisseur.

"Yasuaki-chan's Dead"

It was the first morning of school after the spring vacation. Mr. Kobayashi stood in front of the children assembled on the school grounds, his hands in his pockets as usual. But he didn't say anything for some time. Then he took his hands out of his pockets and looked at the children. He looked as if he had been crying.

"Yasuaki-chan's dead," he said slowly. "We're all going to his funeral today." Then he went on, "You all liked Yasuaki-chan, I know. It's a great shame. I feel terribly sad." He only got that far when his face became bright red and tears welled up in his eyes. The children were stunned and nobody said a word. They were all thinking about Yasuaki-chan. Never had such a sad quietness passed over the grounds of Tomoe before.

"Imagine dying so soon," thought Totto-chan. "I haven't even finished *Uncle Tom's Cabin* that Yasuaki-chan said I ought to read and lent me before the vacation."

She remembered how crooked his fingers had looked when she and Yasuaki-chan said goodbye before spring vacation and he handed her the book. She recalled the first time she met him, when she had asked, "Why do you walk like that?" and his soft reply, "I had polio." She thought of the sound of his voice and his little smile. And that summer tree-climbing adventure of just the two of them. She remembered with nostalgia how heavy his body had been, and the way he had trusted her implicitly even though he was older and taller. It was Yasuaki-chan who told her they had something in America called television. Totto-chan loved Yasuaki-chan. They had lunch together, spent their breaks together, and walked to the station together after school. She would miss him so much. Totto-chan realized that

169

death meant Yasuaki-chan would never come to school any more. It was like those baby chicks. When they died, no matter how she called to them they never moved again.

Yasuaki-chan's funeral took place at a church on the opposite side of Denenchofu from where he lived.

The children walked there in silence from Jiyugaoka, in single file. Totto-chan didn't look around her as she usually did but kept her eyes on the ground the whole time. She realized she now felt differently from when the headmaster had told them the sad news. Her first reaction was disbelief, and then came sadness. But now all she wanted was to see Yasuaki-chan alive just once more. She wanted to talk to him so much she could hardly bear it.

The church was filled with white lilies. Yasuaki-chan's pretty mother and sister and relatives, all dressed in black, were standing outside the church. When they saw Totto-chan they cried even more, their white handkerchiefs in their hands. It was the first time Totto-chan had been to a funeral, and she realized how sad it was. Nobody talked, and the organ played soft hymn music. The sun was shining and the church was full of light, but there was no happiness in it anywhere. A man with a black armband handed a single white flower to each of the Tomoe children and explained that they were to walk one after the other and place their flower in Yasuaki-chan's coffin.

Yasuaki-chan lay in the coffin with his eyes closed, surrounded by flowers. Although he was dead, he looked as kind and clever as ever. Totto-chan knelt and placed her flower by his hand and gently touched it—the beloved hand she had held so often. His hand was so much whiter than her grubby little hand and his fingers so much longer, like a grown-up's.

" 'Bye now," she whispered to Yasuaki-chan. "Maybe we'll meet again somewhere when we're much older. And maybe your polio will be cured by then."

Then Totto-chan got up and looked at Yasuaki-chan once more. "Oh yes, I forgot," she said, "*Uncle Tom's Cabin*. I shan't be able to return it to you now, shall I? I'll keep it for you, until we meet next time."

As she started walking away, she was sure she heard his voice behind her, "Totto-chan, we had a lot of fun together, didn't we? I'll never forget you. Never."

When Totto-chan reached the entrance, she turned around. "I'll never forget you either," she said.

The spring sunshine shone softly just as it had on the day she first met Yasuaki-chan in the classroom-in-the-train. But unlike that day, her cheeks were wet with tears.

A Spy

The children at Tomoe were sad for a long time, thinking about Yasuaki-chan, particularly so in the morning, when it was time to start class. It took a while for the children to get used to the fact that Yasuaki was not just late, but wasn't ever coming again. Small classes might be nice, but at times like this it made things much harder. Yasuaki-chan's absence was so conspicuous. The only saving grace was the fact that seats were not assigned. If he had

171

had a regular desk, its being vacant would have been awful.

Recently Totto-chan had begun to think about what she would like to be when she grew up. When she was younger she thought she wanted to be a street musician or a ballerina, and the day she first arrived at Tomoe she thought it would be nice to be a ticket seller at a station. But now she thought she would like to do some kind of work that was unusual but a little more feminine. It might be rather nice to be a nurse, she thought. But she suddenly remembered that when she had visited the wounded soldiers in the hospital she had noticed nurses doing things like giving injections, and that might be rather difficult. So what should she do? Suddenly she was transported with joy.

"Why, of course! I've already decided what I am going to be!"

She went over to Tai-chan, who had just lit his alcohol burner.

"I'm thinking of becoming a spy," she said proudly.

Tai-chan turned away from the flame and looked at Totto-chan's face for some time. Then he gazed out of the window for a while, as if he were thinking it over, before turning to Totto-chan again to say in his intelligent, resonant voice, slowly and simply, so she would understand, "You have to be clever to be a spy. Besides that, you've got to know a lot of languages."

Tai-chan paused a moment for breath. Then he looked straight at her and said bluntly, "In the first place, a lady spy has to be beautiful."

Totto-chan slowly lowered her eyes from Tai-chan's gaze and hung her head. After a pause, Tai-chan said thoughtfully in a low voice, this time without looking at Totto-chan, "And besides, I don't think a chatterbox could be a spy."

Totto-chan was dumbfounded. Not because he was against her being a spy. But because everything Tai-chan said was true. They were all things she had suspected. She realized then that in every respect she lacked the talents a spy needed. She knew, of course, that Tai-chan had not said those things out of spite. There was nothing to do but give up the idea. It was just as well she had talked it over with him.

"Goodness me," she thought to herself, "Tai-chan's the same age as I am and yet he knows so much more."

Supposing Tai-chan told her he was thinking of being a physicist. What on earth would she be able to say in reply?

She might say, "Well, you're good at lighting alcohol burners with a match." But that would sound too childish.

"Well, you know that *kitsune* is 'fox' in English and *kutsu* are 'shoes,' so I think you could be a physicist." No, that wasn't good enough, either.

In any event, she was quite sure Tai-chan was destined to do something brilliant. So she just said sweetly to Tai-chan, who was watching the bubbles form in his flask, "Thank you. I shan't be a spy, then. But I'm sure you will become somebody important."

Tai-chan mumbled something, scratched his head, and buried himself in the book that lay open before him.

If she couldn't be a spy, then what could she be, wondered Totto-chan, as she stood beside Tai-chan and stared at the flame on his burner.

Daddy's Violin

Before they knew it, the war with all its horrors was beginning to make itself felt in the life of Totto-chan and her family. Every day men and boys from the neighborhood were sent off with waving flags and shouts of "*Banzai!*" Foodstuffs rapidly disappeared one after the other from the shops. It became harder to comply with the Tomoe lunchtime rule of "something from the ocean and something from the hills." Mother was making do with seaweed and pickled plums, but soon even that became difficult to get. Just about everything was rationed. There were no sweets to be found, no matter how hard you searched.

Totto-chan knew about a vending machine under the stairs at Ookayama, the station before hers, where you could get a packet of caramels if you put money in the slot. There was a very appetizing picture on top of the machine. You could get a small packet for five sen and a big one for ten. But the machine had been empty for a long time now. Nothing would come out no matter how much money you put in or how hard you banged. Totto-chan was more persistent than most.

"Maybe there's still one packet in there somewhere," she thought. "Maybe it's caught inside."

So every day she got off the train at the stop before hers and tried putting five- and ten-sen coins into the machine. But all she got back was her money. It fell out with a clatter.

About that time, someone told Daddy what most people would have thought welcome news. If he went and played popular wartime music on his violin at something called a munitions factory—where they made weapons and other things used in war—he would be given sugar and rice and other treats. Since Daddy, who had recently been awarded a prestigious musical decoration, was well known as a violinist, the friend told him he would certainly be given a lot of extra presents.

"What do you think?" Mother asked Daddy. "Are you going to do it?"

Concerts were certainly becoming scarce. In the first place, more and more musicians were being called up and the orchestra was short of players. Radio broadcasts were almost entirely given over to programs connected with the war, so there was not much work for Daddy and his colleagues. He ought to have welcomed the opportunity to play anything.

Daddy thought for some time before replying. "I don't want to play that sort of thing on my violin."

"I think you're right," said Mother. "I would refuse. We'll get food somehow."

Daddy knew Totto-chan had barely enough to eat and was vainly putting money in the caramel vending machine every day. He also knew that the gifts of food he would receive for playing a few wartime tunes would be very handy for his family. But Daddy valued his music even more. Mother knew that, too, and so she never urged him to do it. "Forgive me, Totsky!" said Daddy, sadly.

Totto-chan was too young to know about art and ideology and work. But she did know that Daddy loved the violin so much he had been something called "disowned," and many of his family and relatives did not speak to him any more. He had had a hard time, but he had refused to give up the violin all the same. So Totto-chan thought it quite right for him not to play something he didn't like. Totto-chan skipped about around Daddy and said cheerfully, "I don't mind. Because I love your violin, too."

But the next day Totto-chan again got off at Ookayama and peered into the hole in the vending machine. It was unlikely that anything would come out, but she still kept hoping.

After lunch, when the children put away the chairs and desks that had been arranged in a circle, the Assembly Hall seemed quite spacious.

"Today, I'm going to be the first to climb on the headmaster's back," decided Totto-chan.

That's what she always wanted to do, but if she hesitated for a moment, someone else would have already climbed into his lap as he sat cross-legged in the middle of the Assembly Hall, and at least two others would be scrambling onto his back, clamoring for his attention.

"Hey, stop it, stop it," the headmaster would remonstrate, red in the face with laughter, but once they had occupied his back, the children were determined not to give up their position. So if you were the least bit slow, you'd find the headmaster's back very crowded. But this time Totto-chan made up her mind to be there first and was already waiting in the middle of the Assembly Hall when the headmaster arrived. As he approached, she shouted to him, "Sir, I've got something to tell you."

"What is it, then?" asked the headmaster delightedly, as he sat down on the floor and started to cross his legs.

Totto-chan wanted to tell him what she had decided after several days' thought. When the headmaster had crossed his legs, Totto-chan suddenly decided against climbing on his back. What she had to say would be more appropriate said face to face. So she sat down very close to him, facing him, and tilted her head a little with a smile that Mother had called her "nice face" ever since she was small. It was her

"Sunday best" face. She felt confident when she smiled like that, her mouth slightly open, and she herself believed she was a good girl.

The headmaster looked at her expectantly. "What is it?" he asked again, leaning forward.

Totto-chan said sweetly and slowly, in a big-sisterly or motherly way, "I'd like to teach at this school when I grow up. I really would."

Totto-chan expected the headmaster to smile, but instead, he asked in all seriousness, "Promise?"

He really seemed to want her to do it.

Totto-chan nodded her head vigorously and said, "I promise," determining in her heart to become a teacher there without fail.

At that moment she was thinking about the morning when she first came to Tomoe as a first grader and met the headmaster in his office. It seemed a long time ago. He had listened patiently to her for four hours. She thought of the warmth in his voice when he had said to her, after she had finished talking, "Now you're a pupil of this school." She loved Mr. Kobayashi even more than she had then. And she was determined to work for him and do anything she could to help him.

When she had promised, he smiled delightedly—as usual, showing no embarrassment about his missing teeth. Totto-chan held out her little finger. The headmaster did the same. His little finger looked strong—you could put your faith in it. Totto-chan and the headmaster then made a pledge in the time-honored Japanese way by linking little fingers. The headmaster was smiling. Totto-chan smiled, too, reassured. She was going to be a teacher at Tomoe! What a wonderful thought.

"When I'm a teacher . . . ," she mused. And these were the things that Totto-chan imagined: not too much study; lots of Sports Days, field kitchens, camping, and walks!

The headmaster was delighted. It was hard to imagine Totto-chan grown-up, but he was sure she could be a Tomoe teacher. He thought the Tomoe children would all make good teachers since they were likely to remember what it was like being a child.

There at Tomoe, the headmaster and one of his pupils were making a solemn promise about something that lay ten years or more in the future, when everyone was saying it was only a matter of time before American airplanes loaded with bombs appeared in the skies over Japan.

Rocky Disappears

Lots of soldiers had died, food had become scarce, everyone was living in fear—but summer came as usual. And the sun shone on the nations that were winning as well as on the nations that weren't.

Totto-chan had just returned to Tokyo from her uncle's house in Kamakura.

There was no camping now at Tomoe and no more lovely visits to hot spring resorts. It seemed as if the children would never be able to enjoy a summer vacation as happy as that one. Totto-chan always spent the summer with her cousins at their house in Kamakura, but this year it had been different. An older boy, a relative who used to tell them scary ghost stories, had been called up and had gone to the war. So there were no more ghost stories. And her uncle who used to tell them such interesting tales about his life in America—they never knew whether they were true or not—was at the front. His name was Shuji Taguchi, and he was a top-ranking cameraman.

After serving as bureau chief of Nihon News in New York and as Far East representative of American Metro-News, he was better known as Shu Taguchi. He was Daddy's elder brother, though Daddy had taken his mother's family name in order to perpetuate it. Otherwise Daddy's surname would have been Taguchi, too. Films Uncle Shuji had shot, such as "The Battle of Rabaul," were being shown at movie theaters, but all he sent from the front were his films, so Totto-chan's aunt and cousins were worried about him. War photographers always showed the troops in dangerous positions, so they had to be ahead of the troops to show them advancing. That was what Totto-chan's grown-up relatives had been saying.

Even the beach at Kamakura somehow seemed forlorn that summer. Yat-chan was funny, though, in spite of it all. He was Uncle Shuji's eldest son. Yat-chan was about a year younger than Totto-chan. The children all slept together under one large mosquito net, and before he went to sleep, Yat-chan used to shout "Long Live the Emperor!" then fall like a soldier who had been shot and pretend to be dead. He would do it over and over again. The funny thing was that whenever he did this, he invariably walked in his sleep and fell off the porch, causing a great fuss.

Totto-chan's mother had stayed in Tokyo with

Daddy, who had work to do. Now that summer vacation was over, Totto-chan had been brought back to Tokyo by the sister of the boy who used to tell ghost stories.

As usual on arriving at home, the first thing Totto-chan did was look for Rocky. But he was nowhere to be found. He wasn't in the house and he wasn't in the garden. Nor was he in the greenhouse where Daddy grew orchids. Totto-chan was worried, since Rocky normally came out to meet her long before she even reached the house. Totto-chan went out of the house and down the road, calling his name, but there was no sign of those beloved eyes, ears, or tail. Totto-chan thought he might have gone back while she was out looking for him, so she hurriedly ran home to see. But he wasn't there.

"Where's Rocky?" she asked Mother.

Mother must have known Totto-chan was running everywhere looking for Rocky, but she didn't say a word.

"Where's Rocky?" Totto-chan asked again, pulling Mother's skirt.

Mother seemed to find it difficult to reply. "He disappeared," she said.

Totto-chan refused to believe it. How could he have disappeared? "When?" she asked, looking Mother in the face.

Mother seemed at a loss for words. "Just after you left for Kamakura," she began, sadly. Then she hurriedly continued, "We looked for him. We went everywhere. And we asked everybody. But we couldn't find him. I've been wondering how to tell you. I'm terribly sorry."

Then the truth dawned on Totto-chan. Rocky

must have died. "Mother doesn't want me to be sad," she thought, "but Rocky's dead."

It was quite clear to Totto-chan. Up till now, no matter how long Totto-chan was gone, Rocky never went far from the house. He always knew she would come back. "Rocky would never go off like that without telling me," she thought to herself. It was a strong conviction.

But Totto-chan did not discuss it with Mother. She knew how Mother must feel. "I wonder where he went," was all she said, keeping her eyes lowered.

It was all she could do to say that much, and then she ran upstairs to her room. Without Rocky, the house didn't seem like their house at all. When she

got to her room, she tried hard not to cry and thought about it once more. She wondered whether she had done anything mean to Rocky—anything that would make him want to leave.

"Never tease animals," Mr. Kobayashi always told the children at Tomoe. "It's cruel to betray animals when they trust you. Don't make a dog beg and then not give it anything. The dog won't trust you any more and might develop a bad nature."

Totto-chan always obeyed these rules. She had never deceived Rocky. She had done nothing wrong that she could think of.

Just then Totto-chan noticed something clinging to the leg of her teddy bear on the floor. She had managed not to cry until then, but when she saw it she burst into tears. It was a little tuft of Rocky's light brown hair. It must have come off when the two of them had rolled about on the floor, playing, the morning she left for Kamakura. With those few little German shepherd hairs clutched in her hand, she cried and cried. Her tears and her sobbing just wouldn't stop.

First Yasuaki-chan and now Rocky. Totto-chan had lost another friend.

The Tea Party

Ryo-chan, the janitor at Tomoe, whom all the children liked so much, was finally called up. He was a grown-up, but they all called him by his childish nickname. Ryo-chan was a sort of guardian angel who always came to the rescue and helped when anyone was in trouble. Ryo-chan could do anything. He never said much, and only smiled, but he always knew just what to do. When Totto-chan fell into the cesspool, it was Ryo-chan who came to her rescue straight away, and washed her off without so much as a grumble.

"Let's give Ryo-chan a rousing, send-off tea party" said the headmaster.

"A tea party?"

Green tea is drunk many times during the day in Japan, but it is not associated with entertaining—except ceremonial powdered tea, a different beverage altogether. A "tea party" would be something new at Tomoe. But the children liked the idea. They loved doing things they'd never done before. The children didn't know it, but the headmaster had invented a new word, *sawakai* (tea party), instead of the usual *sobetsukai* (farewell party), on purpose. A farewell party sounded too sad, and the older children would understand that it might really be farewell if Ryo-chan got killed and didn't come back. But nobody had ever been to a tea party before, so they were all excited.

After school, Mr. Kobayashi had the children arrange the desks in a circle in the Assembly Hall just as at lunchtime. When they were all sitting in a circle, he gave each one a single thin strip of roasted dried squid to have with their green tea. Even that was a great luxury in those wartime days. Then he sat down next to Ryo-chan and placed a glass before him with a little saké in it. It was a ration obtainable only for those leaving for the front.

"This is the first tea party at Tomoe," said the headmaster. "Let's all have a good time. If there's anything you'd like to say to Ryo-chan, do so. You can say things to each other, too, not just to Ryo-chan. One by one, standing in the middle."

It was not only the first time they had ever eaten dried squid at Tomoe, but the first time Ryo-chan had sat down with them, and the first time they had seen Ryo-chan sipping saké.

One after the other the children stood up, facing Ryo-chan, and spoke to him. The first children just told him to take care of himself and not get sick. Then Migita, who was in Totto-chan's class, said, "Next time I go home to the country I'll bring you all back some funeral dumplings."

Everyone laughed. It was well over a year since Migita first told them about the dumplings he had once had at a funeral and how good they were. Whenever the opportunity arose, he promised to bring them some, but he never did it.

When the headmaster heard Migita mention funeral dumplings, it gave him quite a start. Normally it would have been considered bad luck to mention funeral dumplings at such a time. But Migita said it so innocently, just wanting to share with his friends something that tasted so good, that the headmaster laughed with the others. Ryo-chan laughed heartily, too. After all, Migita had been telling him for ages that he would bring him some.

Then Oe got up and promised Ryo-chan that he was going to become the best horticulturist in Japan. Oe was the son of the proprietor of an enormous nursery garden in Todoroki. Keiko Aoki got up next and said nothing. She just giggled shyly, as usual, and bowed, and went back to her seat. Whereupon Totto-chan rushed forward and said for her, "The chickens at Keiko-chan's can fly! I saw them the other day!"

Then Amadera spoke. "If you find any injured cats or dogs," he said, "bring them to me and I'll fix them up."

Takahashi was so small he crawled under his desk to get to the center of the circle and was there as quick as a wink. He said in a cheerful voice, "Thank you Ryo-chan. Thank you for everything. For all sorts of things."

Aiko Saisho stood up next. She said, "Ryo-chan, thank you for bandaging me up that time I fell down. I'll never forget." Aiko Saisho's great-uncle was the famous Admiral Togo of the Russo-Japanese War, and Atsuko Saisho, another relative of hers, was a celebrated poetess at Emperor Meiji's court. But Aiko never mentioned them.

Miyo-chan, the headmaster's daughter, knew Ryo-chan the best. Her eyes were full of tears. "Take care of yourself, won't you, Ryo-chan. Let's write to each other."

Totto-chan had so many things she wanted to say she didn't know where to begin. So she just said, "Even though you're gone, Ryo-chan, we'll have a tea party every day."

The headmaster laughed, and so did Ryo-chan. All the children laughed, too, even Totto-chan herself.

But Totto-chan's words came true the very next day. Whenever there was time the children would form a group and play "tea party." Instead of dried squid, they would suck things like tree bark, and they sipped glasses of water instead of tea, sometimes pretending it was saké. Someone would say, "I'll bring you some funeral dumplings," and they'd all laugh. Then they'd talk and tell each other their

186

thoughts. Even though there wasn't anything to eat, the "tea parties" were fun.

The "tea party" was a wonderful farewell gift that Ryo-chan left the children. And although none of them had the faintest idea then, it was in fact the last game they were to play at Tomoe before the children parted and went their separate ways.

Ryo-chan went off on the Toyoko train. His departure coincided with the arrival of the American airplanes. They finally appeared in the skies above Tokyo and began dropping bombs every day.

🌷 Sayonara, Sayonara!

Tomoe burned down. It happened at night. Miyo-chan, her sister Misa-chan, and their mother—who all lived in the house adjoining the school—fled to the Tomoe farm by the pond at Kuhonbutsu Temple and were safe.

Lots of incendiary bombs dropped by the B29 bombers fell on the railroad cars that served as schoolrooms.

The school that had been the headmaster's dream was enveloped in flames. Instead of the sounds he loved so much of children laughing and children singing, the school was collapsing with a fearful noise. The fire, impossible to quench, burned it down to the ground. Fires blazed up all over Jiyugaoka.

In the midst of it all, the headmaster stood in the road and watched Tomoe burn. He was dressed, as usual, in his rather shabby black three-piece suit. He stood with both hands in his jacket pockets.

"What kind of school shall we build next?" he asked his university-student son Tomoe, who stood

187

beside him. Tomoe listened to him dumbfounded.

Mr. Kobayashi's love for children and his passion for teaching were stronger than the flames now enveloping the school. The headmaster was cheerful.

Totto-chan was lying down in a crowded evacuation train, squeezed in amongst adults. The train was headed northeast. As she looked out of the window at the darkness outside, she thought of the headmaster's parting words, "We'll meet again!" and the words he used to say to her time and time again, "You're really a good girl, you know." She didn't want to forget those words. Safe in the thought that soon she would see Mr. Kobayashi again, she fell asleep.

The train rumbled along in the darkness with its load of anxious passengers.

POSTSCRIPT

To write about the school called Tomoe and Sosaku Kobayashi, the man who founded and ran it, is one of the things I have most wanted to do for a long time.

I have invented none of the episodes. They are all events that really happened and, thankfully, I have been able to remember quite a few of them. Besides wanting to write them down, I have been anxious to make amends for a broken pledge. As I have described in one of the chapters, as a child I made a solemn promise to Mr. Kobayashi that I would teach at Tomoe when I grew up. However, it was a promise I was not able to fulfill. Instead I have tried to reveal, to as many people as possible, what sort of man Mr. Kobayashi was, his great love for children, and how he set about educating them.

Mr. Kobayashi died in 1963. If he were alive today there would be much more he could have told me. Even as I write I realize how many episodes that just seem happy childhood memories to me were, in fact, activities carefully thought out by him to achieve certain results. "So that's what Mr. Kobayashi must have had in mind," I find myself thinking. Or, "Fancy him even thinking about that." With each discovery I make, I am amazed—and deeply moved and grateful.

In my own case, I find it impossible to assess how much I have been sustained by the way he used to keep saying to me, "You're really a good girl, you know." Had I not entered Tomoe and had I never met Mr. Kobayashi, I would probably have been labeled "a bad girl," becoming complex-ridden and confused.

Tomoe was destroyed by fire in the Tokyo air raids in 1945. Mr. Kobayashi had built the school with his own money, so reestablishing it took time. After the war, he started a kindergarten on the old site, while helping to establish what is now the Child Education Department of Kunitachi College of Music. He also taught eurythmics there and assisted in the establishment of Kunitachi Elementary School. He died, at the age of sixty-nine, before he could set up his ideal school once more.

Tomoe Gakuen was in southwest Tokyo, a three-minute walk from Jiyugaoka Station on the Toyoko Line. The site is now occupied by the Peacock supermarket and parking lot. I went there the other day out of sheer nostalgia, although I knew nothing was left of the school or its grounds. I drove slowly past the parking lot, where the railroad-car classrooms and playground used to be. The man in charge of the parking lot saw my car and called out, "You can't come in, you can't come in. We're full!"

"I don't want to park," I felt like saying, "I'm just evoking memories." But he would not have understood, so I went on. But a great sadness came over me and tears rolled down my cheeks as I sped away.

I am sure all over the world there are fine educators—people with high ideals and a great love for children—who dream of setting up ideal schools. And I know how difficult it must be to realize this dream. It took Mr. Kobayashi years and years of study before starting Tomoe in 1937 and it burned down in 1945, so its existence was very brief.

I like to believe that the period I was there was when Mr. Kobayashi's enthusiasm was at its height and his schemes in full flower. But when I think how many children could have come under his care had there been no war, I am saddened at the waste.

I have tried to describe Mr. Kobayashi's educational methods in this book. He believed all children are born with an innate good nature, which can be easily damaged by their environment and the wrong adult influences. His aim was to uncover their "good nature" and develop it, so that the children would grow into people with individuality.

Mr. Kobayashi valued naturalness and wanted to let children's characters develop as naturally as possible. He loved nature, too. His younger daughter, Miyo-chan, told me her father used to take her for walks when she was small, saying, "Let's go and look for the rhythms in nature."

He would lead her to a large tree and show her how the leaves and branches swayed in the breeze; he would point out the relationship between the leaves, the branches, and the trunk; and how the swaying of the leaves differed according to whether the wind was strong or weak. They would stand still and observe things like that, and if there was no wind, they would wait patiently, with upturned faces, for the slightest zephyr. They observed not only the wind, but rivers, too. They used to go to the nearby Tama River and watch the water flowing. They never tired of doing things like that, she told me.

Readers may wonder how the authorities in wartime Japan allowed such an unconventional elementary school to exist, where studies were carried out in such an atmosphere of freedom. Mr. Kobayashi hated publicity, and even before the war did not allow photographs of the school or any publicity about its unconventionality. That may have been one reason this small school of under fifty pupils escaped notice and managed to continue. Another was that Mr. Kobayashi was highly regarded at the Ministry of Education as an educator of children.

Every November third—the day of those wonderful Sports Days of fond memory—the pupils of Tomoe, regardless of when they graduated, get together in a room in Kuhonbutsu Temple for a happy reunion. Although we are all in our forties now—many of us are nearing fifty—and have grown children of our own, we still call each other by our nicknames just as in the old days. These reunions are one of the many happy legacies Mr. Kobayashi left us.

It is true that I was expelled from my first elementary school. I do not remember much about that school—my mother told me about the street musicians and the desk. I found it hard to believe I had been expelled. Could I really have been as naughty as all that? However, five years ago I took part in a morning television show in which I was introduced to someone who had known me at that time. She turned out to be the homeroom teacher of the class next to mine. I was dumbfounded at what she told me.

"You were in the room right next to mine," she said, "and when I had to go to the faculty room during class, I usually found you standing in the corridor for some misdemeanor. As I went past, you always stopped me and asked me why you'd been made to stand out there, and what you had done wrong. 'Don't you like street musicians?' you asked me once. I never knew how to deal with you, so finally, even if I wanted to go to the faculty room I would peep out first, and if you were in the corridor I avoided going. Your homeroom teacher often talked about you to me in the faculty room. 'I wonder why she's like that,' she would say. That's why, in later years, when you started appearing on television, I recognized your name immediately. It was a long time ago, but I remember you distinctly when you were in first grade."

Was I made to stand outside in the corridor? I hadn't remembered that and was surprised. It was this youthful-looking, gray-haired teacher with a kindly face, who had taken the trouble to come to an early morning television show, who finally convinced me that I really had been expelled.

And here I would like to express my heartfelt gratitude to my mother for not having told me about it until after my twentieth birthday.

"Do you know why you changed elementary schools?" she asked me one day. When I said no, she went on, quite nonchalantly, "It was because you were expelled."

She might have said at the time, "What's going to become of you? You've already been expelled from one school. If they expel you from the next, where will you go?"

If Mother had spoken to me like that, how wretched and nervous I would have felt as I entered the gate of Tomoe Gakuen on my first day there. That gate with roots and those railroad-car classrooms would not have seemed nearly so delightful to me. How lucky I was to have a mother like mine.

With the war on, only a few photographs were taken at Tomoe. Among them the graduation photographs are the nicest. The graduating class usually had its photograph taken on the steps in front of the Assembly Hall, but when the graduates started lining up with shouts of, "Come on, get in the picture!" other children would want to get in it, too, so it is impossible now to tell which class was graduating. We have animated discussions on the subject at our reunions. Mr. Kobayashi never used to say anything on these picture-taking occasions. Perhaps he thought it was better to have a lively photograph of everyone in the school than a formal graduation picture. Looking at them now, these pictures are very representative of Tomoe.

There is much more I could have written about Tomoe. But I shall be content if I have made people realize how even a little girl like Totto-chan, given the right kind of adult influence, can become a person who is able to get along with others.

I am quite sure that if there were schools now like Tomoe, there would be less of the violence we hear so much of today and fewer school dropouts. At Tomoe nobody wanted to go home when school was over. And in the morning we could hardly wait to get there. It was that kind of school.

Sosaku Kobayashi, the man who had the inspiration and vision to set up this wonderful school, was

194

born on June 18, 1893, in the country northwest of Tokyo. Nature and music were his passions, and as a child he would stand on the bank of the river near his home, with Mount Haruna in the distance, and pretend the gushing waters were an orchestra, which he would "conduct."

He was the youngest son of six children in a rather poor farming family and had to work as an assistant schoolteacher after an elementary education. To obtain the necessary certificate to do it, however, was quite a feat for a boy that age, and it showed exceptional talent. Soon he got a position at an elementary school in Tokyo, and he combined teaching with music studies, which finally enabled him to carry out his cherished ambition and enter the Music Education Department of Japan's foremost conservatory of music—now the Tokyo University of Fine Arts and Music. On graduation, he became music instructor at Seikei Elementary School, founded by Haruji Nakamura, a wonderful man who believed a child's elementary education was of the utmost importance. He kept classes small and advocated a sufficiently free curriculum to bring out the child's individuality and promote self-respect. Study was done in the mornings. Afternoons were devoted to walks, plant collecting, sketching, singing, and listening to discourses by the headmaster. Mr. Kobayashi was greatly influenced by his methods and later instituted a similar kind of curriculum at Tomoe.

While teaching music there, Mr. Kobayashi wrote a children's operetta for the students to perform. The operetta impressed the industrialist Baron Iwasaki, whose family founded the giant business enterprise Mitsubishi. Baron Iwasaki was a patron of the arts—helping Kosçak Yamada, doyen of Japanese composers, as well as giving financial support to the school. The baron offered to send Mr. Kobayashi to Europe to study educational methods.

Mr. Kobayashi spent two years in Europe, from 1922 to 1924, visiting schools and studying eurythmics with Emile Jaques-Dalcroze in Paris. On his return, he established Seijo Kindergarten with another man. Mr. Kobayashi used to tell the kindergarten teachers not to try and fit the children into preconceived molds. "Leave them to nature," he would say. "Don't cramp their ambitions. Their dreams are bigger than yours." There had never been a kindergarten like it in Japan.

In 1930, Mr. Kobayashi set off for Europe for a further year of study with Dalcroze, traveling around and making observations, and decided to start his own school on returning to Japan.

Besides starting Tomoe Gakuen in 1937, he also established the Japan Eurythmics Association. Most people remember him as the man who introduced eurythmics to Japan and for his work in connection with Kunitachi College of Music after the war. There are very few of us left who directly experienced his methods of teaching, and it is a tragedy that he died before he was able to establish another school like Tomoe. Even as it burned, he was already envisaging a better school. "What kind of school shall we build next?" he asked, in high spirits, undaunted by the commotion around him.

When I began writing this book, I was amazed to find that the producer of "Tetsuko's Room," my daily television interview program—a producer I had worked with for years—had been doing research on Mr. Kobayashi for a decade. He had never met the educator, but his interest was aroused by a woman who once played the piano for children's eurythmics classes. "Children don't walk like that, you know," Mr. Kobayashi had said, correcting her tempo, when she first began. Here was a man who was so attuned to children that he knew how they breathed and how they moved. I am hoping Kazuhiko Sano, my producer, will write his book soon to tell the world a great deal more about this remarkable man.

Twenty years ago an enterprising young Kodansha editor noticed an essay I had written about Tomoe in a women's magazine. He came to see me, armed with a great many pads of paper, asking me to expand the material into a book. I guiltily used the paper for something else, and the young man became a director before his idea materialized. But it was he, Katsuhisa Kato, who gave me the idea—and the confidence—to do it. Not having written much then, a whole book seemed daunting. In the end, I was induced to write a chapter at a time as a series of articles for Kodansha's *Young Woman* magazine, which I did from February 1979 to December 1980.

Every month I would visit the Chihiro Iwasaki Museum of Picture Books in Shimo-shakuji, Nerima-ku, Tokyo, to select an illustration. Chihiro Iwasaki was a genius at depicting children, and I doubt if any artist anywhere in the world could draw children in as lively a way as she. She captured them in their myriad moods and attitudes and could differentiate between a baby of six months and one of nine. I cannot tell you how happy I am to have been able to use her drawings for my book. It is quite uncanny how

197

well they fit my narrative. She died in 1974, but people constantly ask me whether I started writing my book while she was still alive, which shows how true to life her paintings are and the tremendous variety of ways in which she depicted children.

Chihiro Iwasaki left nearly seven thousand pictures, and I was privileged to see a great many of her original paintings through the kindness of her son, who is assistant curator of the museum, and his wife. I extend my gratitude to the artist's husband for permission to reproduce her work. I am also grateful to playwright Tadasu Iizawa, curator of the museum, of which I am now a trustee, who kept urging me to start writing when I procrastinated.

Miyo-chan and all my Tomoe friends were naturally a tremendous help. Heartfelt thanks, too, to my editor of the Japanese edition, Keiko Iwamoto, who kept saying, "We must make this a really splendid book!"

I got the idea for the Japanese title from an expression popular a few years ago that referred to people being "over by the window," meaning they were on the fringe or out in the cold. Although I used to stand at the window out of choice, hoping to see the street musicians, I truly felt "over by the window" at that first school—alienated and very much out in the cold. The title has these overtones, as well as one more—the window of happiness that finally opened for me at Tomoe.

Tomoe is no longer. But if it lives for a little while in your imagination as you read this book, nothing could give me greater joy.

*

Many things have happened during the year that has elapsed between the publication of this book in Japanese and its appearance in English. First of all, the book became an unexpected best seller. Little Totto-chan made Japanese publishing history by selling 4,500,000 copies in a single year.

Next, I was amazed to find it being read as an educational textbook. I had hoped it would be instructive for schoolteachers and young mothers to know that there was once a headmaster like Mr. Kobayashi. But I never imagined the book would have the impact it did. Perhaps it is an indication of how deeply people throughout Japan are concerned about the state of education today.

To children it is a storybook. The many replies from readers polled indicate that in spite of all the difficult words in it, children from the age of seven are reading my book with the aid of a dictionary. I can't tell you how happy this makes me. A Japanese literature scholar, aged one hundred and three, wrote, "I enjoyed it immensely." But far more remarkable is the fact that young children are actually reading it looking up the difficult words when comics and picture books are all the rage and youngsters are said to be no longer interested in the written word.

After the book appeared, I was deluged with requests from film, television, theater, and film animation companies for permission to produce my story in their various mediums. But since so many people had read the book and already formed their own mental images, I felt it would be difficult to improve on their imagination no matter how brilliant the director, so I turned them all down.

But I did agree to an orchestral interpretation because music gives free rein to fantasy. I asked Akihiro Komori—well known for his beautiful music—to undertake the composition. The symphonic tale *Totto-chan: The Little Girl at the Window*, for which I did the narration, was a brilliant success, filling the hall alternately with laughter and tears. A record has been made of it.

The book has now also become official teaching material. With the approval of the Ministry of Education, the chapter "The Farming Teacher" will be used in third grade Japanese language studies starting next year, and the chapter "Shabby Old School" in fourth grade ethics and manners classes. Many teachers are already using the book in their own way. In art classes, for instance, I hear teachers are reading children one of the chapters and then having them draw pictures of what impressed them most.

I have been able to realize my long-cherished dream of founding Japan's first professional theater of the deaf, thanks to royalties from the book—for which I received the Non-Fiction Prize as well as three other awards. For services to society, I recently had the honor of being invited, together with many distinguished guests, including Nobel Prizewinner for Chemistry Ken'ichi Fukui, to the emperor's spring garden party, where I was privileged to have a very pleasant conversation with His Majesty. And last year, I received a commendation from the prime minister to commemorate the International Year of Disabled Persons. The book I wanted to write so much brought all these happy events to pass.

Finally, I would like to express my heartfelt thanks

to Dorothy Britton for translating my book into English. I am very fortunate to have found such a splendid translator. The fact that she is both a musician and a poet has enabled her to put my text into English that has both rhythm and sensitivity and is a delight to read.

Yes, one thing more. I would also like to thank Broadway composer Harold Rome and his author wife, Florence. I had only completed the first chapter when they began urging me to publish my story in English.

TETSUKO KUROYANAGI

Tokyo, 1982

EPILOGUE

What are they doing now, those friends of mine who "traveled" together with me on the same classroom "train?"

Akira Takahashi
Takahashi, who won all the prizes on Sports Day, never grew any taller, but entered, with flying colors, a high school famous in Japan for its rugby team. He went on to Meiji University and a degree in electronic engineering.

He is now personnel manager of a large electronics company near Lake Hamana in central Japan. He is responsible for harmony in the work force and he listens to complaints and troubles and settles disputes. Having suffered much himself, he can readily understand other people's problems, and his sunny disposition and attractive personality must be a great help, too. As a technical specialist, he also trains the younger men in the use of the large machines with integrated circuitry.

I went to Hamamatsu to see Takahashi and his wife—a kindly woman who understands him perfectly and has heard so much about Tomoe she says it is almost as if she had gone there herself. She assured me Takahashi has no complexes whatever about his dwarfism. I am quite sure she is right. Complexes would have made life very difficult for him at the prestigious high school and university he attended, and would hardly enable him to work as he does in a personnel department.

Describing his first day at Tomoe, Takahashi said he immediately felt at ease when he saw there were others with physical handicaps. From that moment he suffered no qualms and enjoyed each day so much he never even once wanted to stay home. He told me he was embarrassed at first about swimming naked in the pool, but as he took off his clothes one by one, so he shed his shyness and sense of shame bit by bit. He even got so he did not mind standing up in front of the others to make his lunchtime speeches.

He told me how Mr. Kobayashi had encouraged him to jump over vaulting-horses higher than he was, always assuring him he could do it, although he suspects now that Mr. Kobayashi probably helped him over them—but not until the very last moment, letting him think he had done it all by himself. Mr. Kobayashi gave him confidence and enabled him to know the indescribable joy of successful achievement. Whenever he tried to hide in the background, the headmaster invariably brought him forward so he had to develop a positive attitude to life willy-nilly. He still remembers the elation he felt at winning all those prizes. Bright-eyed and sensible as ever, he reminisced happily about Tomoe.

A good home environment must have contributed, too, to Takahashi's developing into such a fine person. Nevertheless, there is no doubt about the fact that Mr. Kobayashi dealt with us all in a very far-sighted way. Like his constantly saying to me, "You're really a good girl, you know," the encouraging way he kept saying to Takahashi, "You can do it!" was a decisive factor in shaping his life.

As I was leaving Hamamatsu, Takahashi told me something I had completely forgotten. He said he was often teased and bullied by children from other schools on his way to Tomoe and would arrive there crestfallen, whereupon I would quickly ask him what children had done it and was out of the gate in a flash. After a while I would come running back and assure him it was all right now and wouldn't happen again.

"You made me so happy then," he said when we parted. I had forgotten. Thank you, Takahashi, for remembering.

Miyo-chan (Miyo Kaneko)
Mr. Kobayashi's third daughter, Miyo-chan, graduated from the Education Department of Kunitachi College of Music and now teaches music at the elementary school attached to the college. Like her father, she loves teaching young children. From the time she was about three years old, Mr. Kobayashi had observed Miyo-chan walking and moving her body in time to music, as well as learning to talk, and this helped him greatly in his teaching of children.

Sakko Matsuyama (now Mrs. Saito)
Sakko-chan, the girl with the large eyes who was wearing a pinafore with a rabbit on it the day I started at Tomoe, entered a school that was in those days very difficult for girls to get into—now known as Mita High School. She went on to the English

Department of Tokyo Woman's Christian University, became an English instructor with the YWCA, and is still there. She makes good use of her Tomoe experience at their summer camps.

She married a man she met while climbing Mount Hotaka in the Japan Alps. They named their son Yasutaka—the last part commemorating the name of the mountain on which they met.

Taiji Yamanouchi
Tai-chan, who said he wouldn't marry me, became one of Japan's leading physicists. He lives in America, an example of the "brain drain." He graduated in physics from the Science Department of Tokyo University of Education. After his M.Sc., he went to America on a Fulbright exchange scholarship and got his doctorate five years later at the University of Rochester. He remained there, doing research in experimental high-energy physics. At present he is at the Fermi National Accelerator Laboratory in Illinois, the world's largest, where he is assistant director. It is a research laboratory comprising the cleverest people from fifty-three universities in America, and is a giant organization with 145 physicists and 1,400 technical staff, so you can see what a genius Tai-chan is. The laboratory attracted world attention five years ago when it succeeded in producing a high-energy beam of 500 billion electron volts.

Recently, Tai-chan, in collaboration with a professor from Columbia University, discovered something called upsilon. I am sure Tai-chan will receive the Nobel Prize one day.

Tai-chan married a talented girl who graduated

with honors in mathematics from the University of Rochester. With such brains, Tai-chan would probably have gone far no matter what elementary school he attended. But I think the Tomoe system of letting children work on subjects in any order they wanted probably helped to develop his talent. I cannot remember him doing anything during class but working with his alcohol burner and his flasks and test tubes or reading terribly difficult-looking books on science and physics.

Kunio Oe

Oe, the boy who pulled my braids, is now Japan's foremost authority on Far Eastern orchids, whose bulbs can cost tens of thousands of dollars. His is a very specialized field, and Oe is in great demand and constantly travels all over Japan. It was with difficulty that I managed to get hold of him by telephone in between trips and have the following brief conversation:

"Where did you go to school after Tomoe?"

"I didn't go anywhere."

"You didn't go anywhere else? Tomoe was your only school?"

"That's right."

"Good heavens! Didn't you even go to secondary school?"

"Oh yes, I did spend a few months at Oita Secondary School when I was evacuated to Kyushu."

"But isn't finishing secondary school compulsory?"

"That's right. But I didn't."

"My! How happy-go-lucky he is," I thought. Before the war, Oe's father owned an enormous nursery garden that encompassed most of the area called Todoroki in southwest Tokyo, but it was all destroyed in the bombing. Oe's placid nature was evident in the rest of our conversation as he changed the subject.

"Do you know what's the most fragrant flower? To my mind it's the Chinese spring orchid (*Cymbidium virescens*). No perfume can match it."

"Are they expensive?"

"Some are and some aren't."

"What do they look like?"

"Well, they're not a bit showy. They're rather subdued. But that's their charm."

He hadn't changed a bit since he was at Tomoe. Listening to Oe's relaxed voice I thought, "It doesn't bother him one bit, the fact that he never even graduated from secondary school! He just does his own thing and really believes in himself." I couldn't help being impressed.

Kazuo Amadera

Amadera, who loved animals, wanted to be a vet when he grew up and have a farm. Unfortunately, his father died suddenly, and he had to drastically alter the course of his life, leaving Nihon University's School of Veterinary Medicine and Animal Husbandry to take a job at Keio Hospital. At present he is at the Central Hospital of the Self-Defense Force in a responsible position connected with clinical examination.

Aiko Saisho (now Mrs. Tanaka)

Aiko Saisho, whose great-uncle was Admiral Togo, transferred to Tomoe from the elementary school attached to Aoyama Gakuin. I used to think of her in those days as a very sedate and proper young lady. She probably seemed that way because she had lost her father—a major in the Third Guards Regiment —who was killed during the Manchurian Incident.

After graduating from Kamakura Girls' High School, Aiko married an architect. Now that both her sons are grown and in business, she spends much of her leisure writing poetry.

"So you're carrying on the tradition of your famous aunt who was a poetess laureate at Emperor Meiji's court!" I said.

"Oh, no!" she replied, with an embarrassed laugh.

"You're as modest as you were at Tomoe," I said, "and as ladylike." To which she ventured by way of reply, "You know, my figure's the same now as when I played Benkei!"

Her voice made me think what a warm, happy household hers must be.

Keiko Aoki (now Mrs. Kuwabara)

Keiko-chan, who had the chickens that could fly, is now married to a teacher at Keio University's elementary school. She has a married daughter.

Yoichi Migita

Migita, the boy who kept promising to bring those funeral dumplings, took a degree in horticulture, but he had always liked drawing so he went back to college and graduated from Musashino College of Fine Arts. Now he runs his own graphic design company.

Ryo-chan

Ryo-chan, the janitor, who went off to war, came home safe and sound. He never fails to attend the Tomoe reunions every November third.

NOTES

p. 9　**5** was reluctant to するのをいやがった　**6** clutching 手に
しっかりとにぎっている　**13** snatched away ひったくった
15 longingly ものほしそうに

p. 10　**5** plump 丸々とした　**19** be in charge of の世話係となる
21 occurred to 思いついた　**27** what if だとしたらど
うだったろう　**29** chattering to herself 早口でひとりごとを
言いながら　**33** go about advertising 宣伝をして歩く

p. 11　**1** a touch of despair 絶望のひびき　**6** coming into view
見えてくる　**10** expelled 退学させられて　**14** came
straight to the point 単刀直入に言った　**15** disrupts かき
乱す　**17** tether 限界　**18** was taken aback びっくり
ぎょうてんした　**18** on earth 一体全体　**21** blinking
nervously 神経質そうにまばたきをして　**22** pageboy style
内巻きにした　**30** say まあ, たとえば　**32** bangs down
バタンとおろす

p. 12　**6** put away かたずける　**6** all at top speed ものすごい速
さで　**7** every single item 一つ一つを　**11** goes
through it all again 同じことをまた繰り返す　**13** It
makes my head spin. めまいがする.　**17** reliving the
scene 場面を再現する　**18** dawned on Mother お母さんにわ
かってきた　**26** pictured 想像してみた　**28** all that
naughty そんなにわるい　**29** novelty もの珍しさ
32 voice rose in pitch 声の調子が高くなった　**34** flinched ひるんでしまった

p. 13　**2** all through class 授業中ずっと　**8** almost shrieked 叫ぶ
ような声で言った　**13** she might just as well stay there
そこにいたってかまわないだろう　**15** garishly dressed 派手な
かっこうをした　**17** tribulation 苦難　**19** in between
[the classroom and the street]　**22** whereupon すると
29 put on a rousing performance 盛大な演奏をしてみせる
31 could do little but する以外ほとんどすることがなかった
32 din やかましい音

p. 14　**4** it would be such a shame だったら困るじゃない
6 disruptive 破壊的な　**8** sympathize with 同情する
10 with a sinking feeling 沈んだ気持になって　**15** composed herself 気が落ち着いた　**17** went on with the

209

lesson 授業を続けた　　23　addressing に声をかけている
31　classroom eaves 教室のひさし

p. 15　3　apologize あやまる　　4　the drawing class episode 図画の
時間のできごと　　7　navy flag 海軍の旗　　10　fringe ふさ
11　banner 旗

p. 16　4　made hundreds of strokes たくさんの筋をかいた
7　marks きずあと　　7　wouldn't come off どうしても消えな
い　　8　rubbed ごしごしこすった　　10　puzzled 困ってしま
って　　14　flagpole 旗ざお　　21　a sort of parting shot 捨
てぜりふみたいに　　25　obviously 明らかに　　30　on
their way to に向っている　　34　what she had done wrong
どんな悪いことをしたのか

p. 17　1　get any complexes ひけめを感じる　　15　pillars 柱
16　in large characters 大きな字で　　22　gateposts 門柱
23　put her head to one side 首をかしげる　　25　askew
斜めに　　28　caught a glimpse of ちらっと見た　　30　squatted down しゃがみ込んだ　　31　shrubbery かん木

p. 18　3　for its classrooms 教室用に　　4　abandoned いらなくなっ
た　　7　sparkled きらきら輝いていた　　12　let out a
whoop of joy 喜びの声をあげた　　16　startled びっくりして
18　caught hold of つかまえた　　20　holding her back トッ
トちゃんをしっかりおさえて　　28　right away すぐにそのまま

p. 19　2　let go of をはなした　　6　the not very spacious school
grounds あまり広くない校庭　　12　semicircular flight of
about seven stone steps 7段ばかりの半円形の石段
15　abruptly 突然　　15　almost causing～to run into . . .
にぶつかりそうになって　　21　in all seriousness まじめくさっ
て　　22　stationmaster 駅長さん　　23　patience 忍耐

p. 20　8　solid がっしりした　　9　neatly dressed きちんと着こなして
9　shabby 粗末な　　11　spiritedly 元気よく　　14　was embarrassed めんくらった　　23　had a moment's uneasiness
ちょっと不安な様子をした　　31　anything at all you want
to talk about 何でもいいから話したいこと

p. 21　5　higgledy-piggledy むちゃくちゃな　　5　for all she was
worth 一生懸命になって　　12　snip-snip チョキチョキと
15　blew her nose 鼻をかんだ　　19　nod うなずく
21　ran out of things to say 話のたねがなくなった
27　racking her brains 脳みそをしぼって　　33　rips ほころび

p. 22　1　in shreds 裂けて糸みたいになって　　4　barbed wire 鉄条
網　　10　embroidered ししゅうのある　　11　in bad taste
趣味の悪い　　23　yawned あくびをした

p. 23　1　four solid hours まるまる4時間　　8　were at their

210

wit's end to know what to do どうしていいのかわからなかった **9** a naturally sunny disposition 生れつき明るい性格 **11** an air of innocence むじゃきな感じ **23** the Assembly Hall 講堂 **27** tugged at the headmaster's jacket 校長先生の上衣をぐいっと引っぱった

p. 24 **9** something from the ocean 海のもの **10** something from the hills 山のもの **15** squealed with delight 喜びの声をキーキーあげた **23** made Totto-chan so happy [that] she wanted to jump for joy トットちゃんはうれしくなってとびあがりたくなった **25** inspected the lunchboxes おべんとうを見てまわった

p. 25 **3** with her schoolbag strapped to her back ランドセルをしょって **5** viewed Totto-chan's unusual behavior with suspicion トットちゃんのいつもとちがうやり方をいぶかしげにながめた **6** after a good stretch 大きくのびをしてから **15** his hair all tousled もしゃもしゃの髪で **19** tears welled up 涙がわきでてきた **21** vivacious 活発な **23** fervently 熱烈に **27** decided to say nothing but wait 何も言わずに待っていることにした **30** squatted down しゃがんだ

p. 26 **4** ears pointed 耳をぴんと立てて **5** after giving the pass a few licks 定期券をちょっとなめてから **5** yawned あくびをした **14** took the cord with the pass off Rocky's neck 定期券のひもをロッキーの首からはずした **18** her bag flapping against her back ランドセルを背中でパタパタさせながら **26** decided not to [show it] 見せないことにした **31** looking mystified けげんそうな顔をして

p. 27 **5** whimpered くんくん鳴いた **14** with excitement 興奮のあまり **16** a perpetual journey 永遠の旅 **17** baggage racks あみ棚 **24** resembled 似ていた **27** made a firm decision to する固い決心をした **31** stationary 動かない

p. 28 **12** stood on tiptoe つま先で立った **17** Bad shot! はずれ **18** taking aim ねらいをつけて **20** scrambled onto the desk 机の上にやっとこさのっかった **22** his failure to do this first 最初にうまくできなかったこと **22** made it count as a miss 失敗ということになった **30** seating arrangements 席順

p. 29 **4** after a lot of thought and a good look around ゆっくり考えて、まわりをゆっくり見まわしてから **7** pinafore 袖なし簡単服 **10** schedule one subject 1課目だけをやる **23** a small explosion was liable to occur いつ小爆発が起こるか知れなかった **25** enabled the teachers to observe 先生は〜をよく見ることができた **26** as the children prog-

211

ressed to higher grades 生徒が進級するに従って　　　**30**　as for the pupils 生徒にとって　　**32**　cope with 処理する **34**　mostly independent 自習で

p. 30　**1**　whenever necessary 必要なときはいつでも　　**5**　in the truest sense of the word 本当の意味での　　**7**　inattentively ぼんやりして　　**13**　calisthenics 体操　　**23**　with her chin cupped in her hands ほおづえをついて　　**25**　swayed dreadfully ひどくゆれた　　**27**　on purpose わざと

p. 31　**2**　polio 小児麻痺　　**8**　stuck together くっついて **9**　concerned 心配になって　　**10**　became embarrassed 困ってしまった　　**28**　a balanced meal 栄養のバランスのとれた食事　　**29**　in addition to your rice ご飯のほかに **32**　nutritiously 栄養的に

p. 32　**5**　crustaceans 甲殻類

p. 33　**2**　be extravagant ぜいたくをする　　**2**　two requirements 二つの条件（つまり，山のものと海のもの）　　**9**　so enviously とてもうらやましそうに　　**18**　made his round of inspection 見てまわった　　**22**　dole out 分けてあげる　　**26**　no one would have dreamed of saying ... any more than thinking 〜と考えることはおろか…と言おうなどとは考えつきもしなかった **32**　in good spirits おおよろこびで

p. 34　**5**　it was all she could do to するのがせいいっぱいだった **9**　cod roe たらこ　　**20**　addressed the whole school 生徒全員に言った　　**30**　scraping the flesh 肉をそぎおとす

p. 35　**2**　the whole school trooped over　生徒全員がぞろぞろやって来た　　**8**　sniffed at においをくんくんかいだ　　**11**　it was fascinating wondering と考えるのは素敵だった　　**15**　all in all 大休において　　**16**　contentedly 満足して　　**28**　round 輪唱

p. 36　**4**　it wasn't until they had finished singing this song that この歌を歌い終ってから　　**16**　at the tops of their voices 大声を出して　　**17**　settled down to にとりかかった **28**　a unanimous shout 全員一致の叫び声

p. 37　**3**　was astounded びっくりした　　**15**　were lined with large cherry trees 大きな桜の木が両側に植わっていた **26**　a shooting star 流れ星　　**30**　was filled with the fluttering of butterflies 蝶々がたくさん飛んでいた

p. 38　**1**　pistils and stamens メシベとオシベ　　**2**　crouched by the road 道のわきにしゃがんだ　　**8**　pistols メシベ (pistils) のもじり〔原文はオシベとアカンベをもじっている〕　　**12**　pitch dark まっ暗

p. 39　**4**　the bare bellies of the two Deva Kings 仁王さまのむき出

212

しのおなか　　**12**　played hopscotch to their hearts' content 満足するまで石けりをした

p. 40　**3**　so eager was she to go to school that とても学校に行きたかったので　　**4**　mornings never dawned soon enough 朝が早く来すぎることはなかった　　**10**　afternoon snack おやつ　　**13**　rejoiced to think と考えてうれしかった　　**25**　all set and "on your marks" すっかりヨーイドンのかっこうをして　　**28**　in a flash あっと言う間に　　**30**　come to a proper halt ちゃんと止まる

p. 41　**6**　pensively 考え深げに　　**27**　filed out to return to their classroom 一団となって教室にもどった　　**28**　a notice requiring everyone to assemble in the school grounds 全員校庭に集まるという指示　　**30**　all agog 期待でわくわくして　　**33**　five parallel lines 五線

p. 42　**8**　after a brief pause 少したってから　　**15**　flushed 顔を赤くして　　**21**　proceeded to wipe it off さっさと消してしまった　　**23**　had something a bit more impressive in mind もう少し心に訴えるようなものを想像していた

p. 43　**13**　taffeta タフタ, リボン地　　**15**　over the triangular flap of the fastening 三角形のふたの上に　　**19**　made it a point to 必らず〜した　　**23**　flush systems 水洗式　　**24**　cesspool 汚水だめ, 便壺　　**30**　before she knew it 知らぬ間に

p. 44　**5**　give up the purse as lost おさいふのことはあきらめる　　**6**　janitor 用務員　　**7**　ladle ひしゃく　　**9**　that did not deter her in the least そんなことぐらいでトットちゃんは全然ひるまなかった　　**13**　after searching in vain 探してもだめだとわかると　　**24**　in danger of falling in herself 自分の方が落ちてしまう危険がある　　**26**　hope for the best 望みは捨てないで　　**34**　having gone so far ここまでやったのだから

p. 45　**1**　with renewed vigor また前よりも元気を出して　　**8**　his hands clasped behind his back as was his habit いつものくせで, 両手を後ろに組んで　　**26**　the liquid portion 水分　　**28**　figure out 考えつく

p. 46　**3**　was undoubtedly due in part to 一部には〜によることはたしかだった　　**28**　exertion 努力

p. 47　**21**　bugs 虫　　**27**　was very upset すっかり面くらった　　**28**　comedians on the radio ラジオの落語家

p. 48　**1**　rectangular with a rounded top 上が丸い長方形　　**2**　carved arabesques 唐草模様の彫刻のある　　**3**　control knobs スイッチのつまみ　　**15**　by way of thanks ありがとうのつもりで　　**16**　Hey, Ma おい, おっ母　　**19**　uproarious-

213

ly 大きな声で　　**23**　an innate sense of humor 生まれつきの
ユーモアのわかる心

p. 49　**8**　branch off this way at that level crossing あの踏切でこっ
ちに分れてくる

p. 50　**1**　derail 脱線する　　**7**　ideas petered out 考えがだんだんなく
なってきた　　**8**　fit on a cart 荷車にうまく乗っかる
19　after much fruitless discussion of one possibility after
another ああでもないこうでもないと大した成果のない議論をした
後　　**24**　it was some while before しばらくしてから
29　they can come back if they like with their pajamas
and a blanket 来たければねまきと毛布を持って来てよい

p. 51　**14**　was afoot 起こるところだった　　**16**　what it was all
about いったいどんな事情なのか　　**27**　after entrusting
their children to the headmaster's care 子供のことを校長先生
にお願いしてから

p. 52　**1**　became drowsy ねむくなった　　**4**　a babel of voices がや
がやという声　　**6**　in the morning haze 朝もやの中に
17　great commotion 大騒ぎ　　**20**　a tremendous operation 大変な大仕事　　**27**　heave-ho, heave-ho ヨイショ、ヨイ
ショ　　**28**　in time to their rhythmic cries 調子のいいかけ
声に合わせて　　**31**　had its wheels removed 車輪をとりはず
してあった

p. 53　**5**　staggering under the onslaught 子供たちにとびつかれてよ
ろめきながら　　**12**　without a stitch on まるっきり何も着な
いで　　**28**　kept stealing glances out of the windows at
the pool 窓の外のプールを盗み見しつづけた　　**29**　littered
with fallen leaves 落葉がちらかって

p. 54　**16**　with shrieks of delight キャーキャー叫びながら
18　stark naked すっぱだかで　　**30**　swimming trunks 水泳
パンツ　　**34**　satisfied herself they could stand みんな立てる
と確信した

p. 55　**2**　as far as you could stretch your arms 手をどんなに伸ばし
ても　　**5**　in their birthday suits 生まれたままの姿で
19　morbidly curious about 変な風に知りたがる
21　take such pains to hide わざわざかくそうとする
27　rid them of feelings of shame はずかしい気持をなくさせ
る　　**29**　inferiority complex 劣等感　　**34**　offspring 子供
たち

p. 56　**6**　became convinced 納得する気持になった　　**19**　once
home 家に着くなり　　**21**　cooling off 涼んでいた
24　report card 通信簿

p. 57　**8**　tilted his head 首をかしげた　　**30**　there's no mention

214

of fares 交通費のことは何も書いてない

p. 58　**2**　for ages 長いこと　**13**　something stiff and starchy 固く ゴワゴワしたもの　**17**　puffing and blowing ふーふー大汗 をかきながら　**18**　before you could say "Jack Robinson" あ っという間に　**34**　happily crawling in and out of this tent and that one あっちのテントこっちのテントに楽しげに出 たり入ったりして

p. 59　**2**　There was much visiting to and fro. あっちこっちで何度 も訪ね合いを行った.　**11**　at times ときどき　**23**　the sound of a scuffle 取っ組み合いの音　**32**　came to pass やっ てきた

p. 60　**8**　the lane leading to Kuhonbutsu 九品仏へ行く道 **10**　a fork about six feet from the ground 地上から2メート ルの高さの二股　**12**　during recess 休み時間に

p. 61　**5**　private property 専有物　**9**　couldn't claim one as his own 自分だけの木をとることができなかった　**12**　make a fuss 大騒ぎする　**18**　parted company 別れた　**21**　her train pass flapping around her neck 定期券を首のまわりにぶら ぶらさせて　**24**　deserted now 今はだれもいない **29**　to steady himself 体のバランスをとるために

p. 62　**6**　the first rung はしごの最初の段　**11**　let alone keep the ladder steady はしごを動かないようにすることはとてもでき ず　**16**　so badly とても　**19**　disconsolate がっかりして **20**　made a funny face おもしろい顔をした　**25**　steplad- der 脚立　**30**　in a big-sisterly voice お姉さんのような声で **31**　wobble ぐらぐらする　**34**　profusely いっぱい

p. 63　**9**　with all his might 全力を尽して　**30**　terribly precarious ひどく不安定な　**34**　mercifully ありがたいことに

p. 64　**6**　bashfully はずかしそうに　**7**　vistas he had never glimpsed before それまで見たこともない遠くの景色 **13**　with enthusiasm 熱心に　**18**　couldn't go very far afield 家からそう遠くへは行けなかった　**23**　all the same そ れでもやっぱり　**26**　cicadas せみ

p. 65　**14**　vied for the privilege 争そって手をあげた　**20**　the re- maining thirty or so children 残りの30名ほどの子供たち **22**　at staggered intervals 少しづつずらして

p. 66　**3**　squealing with excitement 興奮してキーキー叫びながら **26**　reassuring 心が落ち着く

p. 67　**11**　collided head-on 正面衝突した

p. 68　**15**　standing bewildered under street lights 街灯の下でおろお ろして立っている　**18**　weren't frightened of ghosts any more 幽霊が全然こわくなくなった　**22**　sedately おちついて,

215

行儀よく　　**25**　peek in at Daddy's rehearsal hall お父さんの練習場をのぞく　　**29**　ducking under their fences 垣根の下からもぐって

p. 69　**2**　what had intrigued Totto-chan トットちゃんが面白く思ったこと　　**3**　the perspiring conductor 汗びっしょりの指揮者　　**5**　podium指揮台　　**7**　all the rest of the orchestra お父さん以外の楽員全員　　**13**　the representative 代表者　　**13**　as a way of saying thank you ありがとうという意味で　　**16**　unlike school学校とちがって　　**23**　all the way はるばる　　**27**　started persecuting Jews ユダヤ人を迫害しはじめた　　**27**　if it hadn't been for that そんなこと（ユダヤ人迫害）がなかったら　　**32**　through the efforts of の努力のおかげで　　**33**　demanded of the orchestra the same level of オーケストラに同じ水準の要求をした

p. 70　**8**　not deliberate わざとやっているのではなく　　**9**　the intricacies of the situation escaped her トットちゃんにはその場のややこしさはわからなかった　　**16**　hardly daring to breathe 息をひそめて　　**29**　spotted トットちゃんを見かけた

p. 71　**5**　a bit dilapidated こわれかけている　　**8**　the goldfish vendor 金魚売り　　**17**　was flabbergasted びっくりした　　**21**　was filled with admiration すばらしい計画だという気持になった

p. 72　**8**　off we go さあ，行こう　　**11**　were amazingly well behaved とてもお行儀がよかった　　**15**　get in line 一列になる　　**17**　had instilled into them that 〜ということが生徒によくしみ込んでいた　　**33**　embarked on a ship 船に乗った

p. 73　**1**　inspected every corner of the deck 甲板をくまなく探険した　　**4**　the townsfolk on the pier 桟橋にいる町の人たち　　**6**　the sea became very rough 海がとても荒れた　　**8**　amidships 船のまん中で　　**9**　pretending to be a stabilizer 重心をとる物になったつもりで　　**15**　disembarked 下船した

p. 74　**4**　in the regular sea ちゃんとした海で　　**9**　deserted 人がいなくて　　**10**　like being on their own private beach 自分たちだけの浜にいるような　　**11**　enjoyed . . . to the utmost 最高に楽しんだ　　**15**　were tucked into their quilts ふとんの中にもぐり込んだ　　**16**　took turns telling ghost stories 順番におばけの話をした　　**32**　popsicles アイスキャンデー

p. 75　**4**　wood shaving かんなくず　　**7**　had a photograph taken of them all together みんなそろって写真をとってもらった　　**8**　no sooner was the teacher ready with her camera than 先生がカメラを構えるとすぐ　　**25**　crayfish ざりがに　　**26**　the garbageman's cart ごみ屋の荷車

216

p. 76 **3** besides the fact that classes at Tomoe were different from those at ordinary schools トモエの授業が普通の学校とちがうということのほかに　**7** eurythmics リトミック
11 training and research institutes sprang up everywhere 養成所や研究所があちこちに新しくできた　**25** how to awaken a child's sensitivity どのようにして子供の感覚を呼びさますか
27 eventually 結局　**27** the way children jumped and skipped and romped about 子供たちがとんだりはねたり動きまわったりする様子

p. 77 **8** a sport that refines the body's mechanism 体の機構を精巧にする運動　**14** conforming to and obeying the laws of nature 自然の法則に合わせて、それに従う　**19** in time to the music 音楽に合わせて　**21** bump into others ひとにぶつかる　**25** were not supposed to tramp heavily ドシンドシンと歩いてはいけなかった　**26** with toes pointed つま先立って

p. 78 **3** down, around you, out to the sides, and up 下げて、まわして、横から、上に　**5** out in front 前に出して
18 in duple time 2拍子で　**18** the triple rhythm 3拍子
20 cultivate the children's powers of concentration 子供の集中力を養う　**23** with relief ほっとして　**25** be especially alert とくに注意する　**25** in the time it took to ～するのに時間を使っているうちに　**30** groans うなり声
32 thought up variations いろいろ変った形を考えた

p. 79 **1** act in unison いっしょに動く　**4** taboo やってはいけないこと　**12** thereby achieving harmony between the spirit and the flesh そうやって精神と肉体の調和をはかる
13 awakening the imagination and promoting creativity 想像力を呼びおこし、創造性を促進する　**18** an ancient comma-shaped symbol コンマのかっこうをした（つまり巴型の）古い紋　**19** the traditional emblem consisting of two *tomoe* 二つの巴でできた伝統的な紋様　**25** was bound to have good results かならずよい結果を生むはずであった
27 without being affected by too much adult interference 大人の干渉をあまり受けずに　**29** deplored contemporary education 今の教育を嘆かわしいと思っていた

p. 80 **2** atrophy a child's sensual perception 子供の感応的知覚力を萎縮させる　**3** intuitive receptiveness 直観的な感受性

p. 81 **5** not perceiving truth 真実を理解しない　**15** temple fair 縁日　**20** was ablaze with lights 電気で明るくなっていた
21 poked her head inside each of the little stalls 小さな夜店ひとつひとつのぞいた　**23** squeaks ピーという音

217

23 sizzles シュルシュルという音　　**23** pops ポンという音
24 enticing aromas 気をひくにおい　**25** inhaling peppermint はっかを吸い込む　**28** lollipops and cotton candy
べっこう飴とわた飴

p. 82　**1** to make it resound どんぶりがワーンという音をたてるよう
に　**8** yellow baby chicks cheeping away ピヨピヨ鳴いてい
る黄色いひよこ　**13** wiggling their tiny bottoms 小さな尻を
ピクピク動かしながら　**16** quite so appealing そんなに可愛
らしい　**31** had set her heart on に熱中した

p. 83　**5** beseeched her parents 両親にたのんだ　　**7** were adamant けっしてうんといわなかった　**12** sobbing convulsive-
ly しゃくりあげながら　**17** gave in 負けた　**22** slatted
box 桟のついた箱

p. 84　**3** clenched her teeth 歯をくいしばった　**20** without giving their clothes a thought 服のことなど気にせずに
22 anything durable 長もちするもの　**23** patches つぎは
ぎ　**24** the strongest material available 手に入るいちばん丈
夫な生地

p. 85　**1** burrow like a dog 犬のように穴を掘る　**4** quite threadbare すっかり着古した　　**20** heaved a sigh of relief ほっと
して胸をなでおろした　**21** under those circumstances そう
いったやむをえない事情で　**27** a fabrication つくり話
28 go to such lengths to make up an excuse そのようにわ
ざわざ言い訳までしようとする

p. 86　**4** around the rear うしろの方

p. 87　**4** no wonder 何の不思議もなかった　**6** to think that とは
不思議なものだ　**12** clothes they could get as dirty as
they liked 好きなだけ汚せる服　**28** looking forlorn 心細い顔
付をして　**31** affably 愛想よく

p. 88　**8** bounded over to the train 元気よく電車にとび乗った
12 toddled along よちよち動いた　**20** bow-legged がに股
の

p. 89　**1** pulled her eyes out of shape トットちゃんの目をつりあげ
させてしまった　**2** frantically 必死になって　**11** clear
and mature はっきりして大人っぽい　**22** something enticing 面白そうなもの　**26** after a preliminary little hop ちょ
っととんではずみをつけてから　**29** wall plaster 壁土
30 with a "blop" ズボッと音をたてて　**30** gummy stuff
ねちゃねちゃしたもの

p. 90　**3** there was nothing she could do but stay still じっとして
いるほかなかった　**5** gooey mixture ねちゃねちゃした混合物
12 Totto-chan's head sticking out of the pile トットちゃん

218

の頭が壁土の山から突き出ている　**20**　looks intriguing　面白
そうに見える　**32**　cesspool opening　こえだめの汲み取口
34　to keep the smell in　臭いが出ないように

p. 91　**2**　with a great big "plop"　ドボンという大きな音をたてて
9　premature　そう思うのはちょっと早い　**12**　take it into
her head to　しようと思っている　**25**　I gratefully partake
いただきます　**31**　have somebody different each day stand
毎日ちがった人に立ってもらう

p. 92　**7**　was willing to give it a try　（話を）喜んでやってみる気持
があった　**8**　were in favor of the idea　その考えに賛成だっ
た　**11**　as a result of his experience abroad　海外生活の経
験から　**17**　without being embarrassed　はずかしがらずに
25　at any rate　とにもかくにも　**30**　unlike talking to two
or three friends　2,3人の友達と話すのとはちがって

p. 93　**1**　prepared a talk only to forget all of it　せっかくお話を用
意したのに全部忘れてしまった

p. 94　**5**　firmly refused　堅固にお話をするのを拒否した
7　anyone could possibly have nothing to say　言うことが何
もないという子がいるなんて　**17**　heedless of the gaps in
his teeth　歯が抜けていることなど気にせずに　**25**　scratched
his head　頭をかいた

p. 95　**2**　his hands clasped on the desk　両手を机の上にしっかりと
おいて　**3**　That will do.　それでよい.

p. 96　**3**　leaned forward　身を前にのり出した　**7**　clapped　手をたた
いた　**10**　with bated breath　息を殺して　**12**　triumphantly　とくいまんめんに　**31**　a brief tussle　ちょっとじゃれ
つくこと　**31**　bumped into each other　ぶつかりあった

p. 97　**1**　something a little more complicated　もう少しこみ入ったこ
と　**2**　did the deciding　決定をくだした　**5**　the fiercer
wolf face　相手よりも恐ろしい狼の顔　**9**　bare all his teeth　歯
を全部むき出す　**13**　make growling noises　うなり声をあげ
て　**21**　was dangling from her head　（耳が）つけ根からぶ
らさがっていた　**26**　was splattered with blood　血がはねと
んでいた　**30**　pathetically　悲しそうに　**33**　got so
angry with Rocky [that] they got rid of him　ロッキーのこと
を怒って　追い出す

p. 98　**9**　Don't be cross with Rocky!　ロッキーをおこらないで.
13　trickling down　したたり落ちる　**19**　with Mother
leading the way　お母さんが先に行って　**21**　to her
parents' great relief　両親がほっとしたことには　**29**　admonish the dog　犬をしかる　**30**　as much as to say　と言う
かのように

219

p. 99　**5**　there was no stopping her tears now もう涙をこぼすのを とめることはできなかった　**10**　emerged slowly ゆっくりと姿 を現わした　**25**　after a lot of research いろいろ調べた結果

p. 100　**1**　it was uncanny the way it never rained 雨が降らなかっ たのは不思議だった　**8**　requiring no special or elaborate equipment 特別な，また手のこんだ用具など必要でなく　**11**　large tubular cloth streamers 大きな筒状の布の吹流し——鯉 のぼりのこと　**22**　lose your sense of direction 方向感覚を 失う　**25**　hurriedly burrow inside again いそいでまた中に もぐり込む　**27**　made the carp wriggle 鯉をのたうたせた　**31**　propped up on its side 横にして立てかけて　**32**　rungs はしごの段

p. 101　**3**　with catlike grace 猫のようにするりと　**4**　one's bot-tom could get stuck おしりがひっかかる　**22**　idle chit-chat or nibbling food のんびりと世間話をしたり，食物を食べ たりすること

p. 102　**7**　took on a fresh, fun aspect 新鮮で，面白いものに変った　**10**　a beautiful kaleidoscope 美しい万華鏡　**24**　was very taken with すっかりとりことなった　**28**　rippled in such a lovely grown-up way みごとにおとなっぽい様子でゆれ た

p. 103　**15**　clumsily negotiating them a step at a time 一度に一段ず つ無器用に階段をのぼったりおりたりする　**22**　try as they might どんなにがんばっても　**24**　outrun him 高橋君より速く 走る　**28**　as proud as Punch ひどく得意そうに

p. 104　**1**　giant radish 大根　**2**　burdock root ごぼう　**3**　spinach ほうれん草　**29**　provided food . . . by your own efforts 君たちの力で食事の材料を手に入れたんだ

p. 105　**1**　spicy burdock きんぴらごぼう　**11**　no doubt きっと　**15**　before developing an inferiority complex 劣等感を強くす るよりは　**17**　who knows だれにもわからないことだが

p. 106　**8**　at every opportunity 機会あるごとに　**11**　lean frog やせ 蛙　**14**　fledgling sparrows 羽が生えそろいそうな雀，つまり 巣立つ前の雀の子　**18**　wringing こすり合わせる　**19**　implores your mercy 慈悲を求める　**20**　improvised a melody メロディーをつけた

p. 107　**5**　joined the army as a private 陸軍に入隊したときは二等兵 だった　**6**　earned promotion 昇進した　**15**　a proper haiku ちゃんとした俳句　**17**　didn't quite conform to にかな らずしも会っていなかった　**25**　to illustrate his own thoughts about life and nature 人生と自然について自分の考え をわかりやすく教えるために

p. 108 **7** with a great creaking キーという大きな音をたてて
8 brace herself with her feet 両足でしっかり体を支える
10 facing the way the train was going 電車の進行方向を向いて **14** leaned over 傾いた **20** straightened out 水平になった

p. 109 **2** wholeheartedly 気持よく **8** was pushed and jostled 押されたり、突かれたりした **9** desperately stood her ground そこを動かないように必死になってがんばった
17 while it wouldn't seem like much of a sum それがたいした額でないように思われても **27** after turning over lots of ideas in her mind 心の中であれこれ考えた後
31 damp with perspiration 汗でびっしょりになって

p. 110 **11** a thicket 繁み **22** with the feeling という気持で

p. 111 **9** a mole もぐら **18** stone, paper, scissors ジャンケンポン
20 so she could get a better view もっとよく見えるように
26 burst out laughing 笑いだす **29** came to the conclusion という結論に達した

p. 112 **9** the municipal deaf and dumb school 都立聾啞学校
24 vice-principal 教頭 **28** with a fringe of white hair 白髪の輪がついていて **31** recite classical Chinese-style poems 詩吟を吟ずる

p. 113 **5** executed their famous vendetta 有名な仇討ちを行った
7 pay our respects at their graves 四十七士の墓におまいりする **12** the prospct of という計画 **17** plotted . . . to avenge the honor of their dead master 死んだ主君の仇を討とうと計画をめぐらした **19** grievously wronged あわれにもだまされた **24** give away a single secret 秘密をもらす
26 missing classes and going for a walk 授業をつぶして散歩に出かける **29** taking their leave of the headmaster and the other teachers 校長先生と他の先生方に別れを告げて
32 declaiming と熱をこめて言う

p. 114 **3** firing a constant barrage of を連発しながら
7 a stick of incense 線香

p. 115 **1** A hush fell upon the children. 子供たちはしーんとなった。
4 drifted up ゆらゆらとのぼった **20** a tenement 借家、つまり長屋のこと **23** wore her hair parted down the middle and drawn back into a bun 髪を真中で分けて、後の方で結んでいた

p. 116 **4** a small embankment 小さな土手 **7** untidy hair もじゃもじゃの髪 **11** in an arrogant posture いばったような格好をして **14** was scathing and full of hatred 痛烈で、憎しみに満ちていた **18** in such a spiteful way そのように憎々

221

しげに **22** was perplexed 面くらった

p. 117 **10** spoke ill of for no reason at all 何の理由もなく悪口を言った **20** with its combination of irritation and anxiety いら立ちと心配のまざった調子で **23** was drowned by the sound of a passing train 通過する電車の音にかき消されて **31** braid her hair 髪をおさげに編む

p. 118 **4** with bangs 前髪を切り下げて（オカッパ髪の様子を述べている） **9** with the ends secured by rubber bands 先を輪ゴムでとめて **18** for fear the braids might come undone 編んだ髪がバラバラにならないように **23** exclaimed in unison 一斉に歓声をあげた **33** hang onto them お下げ髪につかまる

p. 119 **5** staggered and fell smack on her bottom よろよろして，まともに尻もちをついた **7** without being dragged to the ground as well 地面にころがされなくても **9** "Heave-ho, heave-ho!" オーエス，オーエス． **28** raising her tear-stained face 涙によごれた顔をあげて **30** terrific 素敵だ **34** nodded approval 同意するようにうなずいた

p. 120 **17** Little girls should be seen and not heard. 女の子はだまっているべきで，おしゃべりをしてはいけない． **19** in spite of all that そういうことがあっても

p. 121 **5** as they parted company 別れ別れになるとき **13** a horse-drawn sleigh 馬ぞり **14** a pure white snowscape 純白の雪景色 **30** bobbing her head 頭を少し下げて

p. 122 **1** hug her トットちゃんを抱きしめる **10** with her knees drawn up トットちゃんにひざをかかえさせて **15** made a whistling sound ヒューヒューという音をたてた **20** the onlookers そばで見ていた人たち **32** instinctively 本能的に

p. 123 **4** greeted their discovery with shouts of joy おたがいの発見を歓声をあげて喜び合った **8** the janitor 用務員 **16** some books are reserved for certain grades 本が学年ごとに分かれている **20** any books at home you think the others would like to read 他の人たちが読みたいと思うような家にある本ならどんな本でも **25** unanimously 満場一致で

p. 124 **3** were overjoyed 大喜びだった **5** looked most entertaining とても面白そうに見えた **8** a jumble of voices 様々な声 **11** swap books 本を交換する **13** reading out the accompanying jingle in a loud singsong 歌詞を大きく歌うような調子の声で読みあげて **18** quick as a wink あっという間に **22** with an old-fashioned Japanese hairdo 昔風の日本髪を結った

222

p. 125 4 were trained to concentrate 集中するよう訓練されていた
8 were absorbed in their books 本に夢中だった
11 breaking wind おならをする 17 knocked him unconscious おムコさんをたたきつけて気絶させた 19 was
always in great demand いつもひっぱりだこだった
21 packed into the train like sardines （カンヅメの）いわし
のように電車の中にいっぱい入り込んで 22 devouring the
books 本をむさぼり読む
p. 126 1 holding out 最後までがまんする 3 holding
themselves in strange contortions 変なかっこうに身をかがめて
7 mad at に怒って 12 the way he had come running
in such a hurry そんなに急いで走ってきたところをみると
15 his nostrils a little dilated 鼻を少しふくらませて
23 to be scrubbed clean ごしごしときれいに洗い流すために
p. 127 1 was being reprimanded 叱られていた 14 the theory
of evolution 進化論 14 appealed to the children 子供たち
の心をとらえた 16 the vestige of a tail called a coccyx
尾骨と呼ばれるしっぽのなごり 21 shaking his head
emphatically 頭を強く横にふって 27 did it occur to you
to ということを思いつかなかったのか
p. 128 4 so children like Takahashi would lose their self-
consciousness 高橋君のような子供が恥ずかしく思わないように
10 beyond the headmaster's comprehension 校長先生には理
解できない（こと） 27 the faculty room 職員室
p. 129 8 all set and ready 位置について "用意"を待っていた
9 burst into bloom 一斉に咲き出す 10 black popeyes
黒出目金 24 in their new status as second graders 新し
く2年生になって 28 an eventful year 充実した年
32 a nuisance 厄介者
p. 130 1 misgivings 心もとなさ 4 regarded . . . dubiously …を
疑いの目でみていた 6 superficially 表面的に 13 vented
his despair by pounding on the headmaster's back 校長先生
の背中をたたいてつらい気持を吐き出した 14 the scab from
a grazed knee flapping すりむいたひざのかさぶたをぶらぶらさ
せて 23 was well acquainted with her back 背中にすっか
りなじんだ 27 a very fine troupe 素晴らしいバレー団
31 effortlessly 楽々と
p. 131 1 spurned all others 他のものを全部よせつけなかった
29 make the arrangements 手配をする 32 longing for
the day となる日を夢見ながら
p. 132 1 amble about to piano or phonograph music ピアノやレコ
ードの音楽に合わせて歩きまわる 7 assume some pose they

223

devised themselves 生徒たちが自分で工夫したポーズをとる
11 a person in agony 苦しんでいる人 **13** the image
Totto-chan cherished in her mind トットちゃんが心に抱いてい
るイメージ **17** plucked up courage 勇気を出した
24 an aquiline nose わし鼻 **32** according to your
fancy 自分の好みにしたがって

p. 133 **11** a short striped cotton work jacket 短い, しま模様のつい
た綿の仕事着 **14** of indigo-dyed cotton with narrow legs
紺色の木綿でできた足の細い **17** a rather dilapidated
straw hat 少しぼろぼろになったむぎわら帽子 **23** full of
wrinkles しわだらけで **29** with a toothy smile 歯を見せて
笑って **31** ev'ry=every **31** fer=for

p. 134 **1** full o' [=of] mustard blossoms 菜の花がいっぱい咲いてい
る **5** Naw=No **6** I ain't no teacher.=I'm not a
teacher. **16** teaching qualifications 教員資格
26 farming implements 農耕機具 **32** weeding 草むしり
34 good hiding places よいかくれ場所

p. 135 **2** taking all the nourishment from the soil 土から栄養分を
とってしまうこと **6** furrows うね **7** fertilizer 肥料
18 his strong gnarled hands 頑丈な, ふしくれだった手
19 attest を証明する **22** were dripping with perspiration 汗をぽたぽたたらしていた **25** an impeccable field 立派
な畑 **27** held that farmer in high esteem その農夫をすっ
かり尊敬した

p. 136 **8** were still enfolded in the very heart of peace 平和の奥深
いところにまだつつまれていた **14** Thunder canyon 等々力
渓谷 **14** field kitchen 飯盒すいさん **26** get it muddled ごちゃごちゃになってしまう **26** could do nothing but
keep on repeating it to herself 口の中でくり返す他なかった

p. 137 **1** on the point of replying 答えそうになって **7** a rallying cry 勝利のときの声 **8** Then it clicked. それからぴんと
きた. **16** once their interest is aroused いったん興味がわく
と **19** all the relevant details この行事に関連したこまごま
したこと **29** stuck close to Mother ぴったりとお母さんに
くっついた

p. 138 **1** quickly put her thumb and index finger to her earlobe
いそいで親指とくすり指を耳たぶにつけた **7** evidence of
kitchen expertise 台所仕事に熟練している証拠 **13** as it
filtered through the tall trees 高い木の間からもれてくると
14 with their knapsacks bulging リュックサックにいっぱいも
のを入れて

p. 139 **3** in booming torrents ゴーゴーと勢いよく **13** it

224

wasn't long before すぐに　　**19**　allotted their various tasks
いろいろな仕事を分担した　　**20**　take charge of を受け持つ
22　was assigned to chopping vegetables　野菜を切るのを割
り当てられた　　**24**　made a mess of the job 仕事のやり方が
めちゃめちゃだった　　**27**　eggplants なす　　**29**　in just the
right bite-sized piecesちょうど食べられる大きさに
30　took it upon herself to . . . …することまで引き受けた

p. 140 **5**　flavoring the pork broth豚汁の味つけ　　**10**　tempting
aromas おいしそうなにおい　　**15**　with its attendant
traumas 料理をするときの苦労もいっしょに　　**16**　ingredients
材料　　**24**　the action she had set her heart upon 前々から
やろうと心に決めていた動作　　**34**　first and foremost 何より
もまず第一に

p. 141 **10**　give a little skip ぴょんとはねる　　**16**　fight the tormentors いじめっ子と戦う　　**20**　as she tried to satisfy her curiosity 好奇心を満たそうとして　　**26**　a trapdoor あげぶた

p. 142 **5**　it knocked all the wind out of her lungs すっかり息がつ
まってしまった　　**13**　the child concerned 実際に問題を起
こした子供　　**20**　complaints and fears voiced by children's parents and other teachers 他の子供の親や他の先生か
ら出た苦情や心配　　**30**　in many respects いろいろな点で

p. 143 **2**　instilled a confidence in herself as "a good girl"彼女の心
の中に「良い子」という自信を植えつけた　　**5**　some escapade
何かのいたずら　　**21**　had luxuriated in the sound of
that word その単語の発音にふけった　　**30**　was sauntering
along ぶらぶらと歩いていた

p. 144 **1**　sounded cross おこっているような声だった　　**6**　stood
dazed びっくりして立っていた　　**10**　The Improper Fraction
仮分数　　**13**　in desperation すっかりやけくそになって
15　maturely大人っぽく　　**16**　the ring 土俵

p. 145 **24**　making a rude noise わーいという声を出して

p. 147 **1**　was indignant すっかり頭にきた　　**3**　reiterated the
boys from the other school 他の学校の男子生徒が繰り返して言
った　　**5**　was so infuriated すっかり怒ってしまった
22　linked arms 腕を組んだ

p. 148 **5**　a daily series of agonies 毎日が苦労の連続　　**8**　could
not escape criticism 非難をまぬがれなかった　　**8**　used to a
more conventional system of education もっと普通の教育の仕
方になれている

p. 149 **1**　couldn't have been a happier one この上なく幸せな表情で
あった　　**7**　very observant とても目ざとい　　**12**　airing
some clothes 着物を虫干しする　　**13**　purple pleated skirt

225

むらさき色のはかま　　**27**　shan't＝shall not　　**34**　the fabric was imported その生地は輸入品だった

p. 150 **1** jiggled her head occasionally ときどき頭をゆすった
4 looked a little distressed 少し悲しそうな顔をした
9 importuned by his daughter 娘にねだられた
13 keeps pestering me about it そのリボンのことで私をずっと責めている　　**26** irrespective of age 年令に関係なく
33 the ribbon she had been so thrilled about トットちゃんがあんなに気に入っていたリボン

p. 151 **8** organized nationally 全国的に組織された　　**13** was representing Tomoe トモエ学園の代表だった　　**20** was relieved ほっとした　　**31** wholeheartedly 真心をこめて

p. 152 **6** feeling rather awkward ちょっとばつの悪い思いで
18 started beating time again また拍子をとりはじめた
23 felt very apologetic とても申し訳ない気持になった
28 something . . . that wasn't according to plan 計画にないようなこと

p. 153 **32** as best she could 力いっぱい

p. 154 **6** engulf these very children これらの子供たちをまきこむ
10 well underway もうすっかりはじまって　　**18** what looked like pieces of tree bark 木の皮みたいなもの　　**27** if it tastes bitter もし苦い味だったら

p. 155 **11** vigorously すごいいきおいで　　**18** a real bargain 本当に安い買い物だ　　**27** the moment she got to her classroom 教室につくとすぐに

p. 156 **8** made her way to the office 校長室へ行った　　**30** extolling his product in a loud patter 大声で品物の宣伝をして

p. 157 **11** as fit as a fiddle ぴんぴんしている　　**12** the precious bark wrapped in newspaper 新聞紙につつんだ大切な木の皮

p. 158 **5** hooray＝hurrah　　**17** made no attempt しようともしなかった　　**28** thrust out the tree bark 木の皮をさし出した

p. 159 **2** studied it carefully その皮を注意深く眺めた
3 concerned 不安になって　　**32** 'cause＝because

p. 160 **23** take his time over his studies ゆっくり勉強する
28 in a big-brotherly voice お兄さんのような声で

p. 161 **3** I'll leave him with you 君たちにまかせるよ　　**9** Then what did he do but start to walk into the house with his shoes on! 何とくつをはいたまま家の中に入ったのだ.
26 clustered around him 宮崎君のまわりに集まった
31 pale flesh-colored pinks うすい肉色のピンク

p. 162 **3** a dog pulling a baby by its diaper 犬が赤ちゃんのおむつを引っ張っている　　**9** sociable 人なつっこい　　**13** listened enraptured うっとりと聞きほれた　　**13** began to grapple with Japanese 日本語と格闘しはじめた　　**27** tutor 家庭教師 **34** had become an enemy 敵国になっていた

p. 163 **10** put on a play 劇を上演する　　**17** apart from は別として　　**29** the commander 関守　　**31** is disguised as a porter 荷物かつぎに変装している

p. 164 **1** strolling monks 山伏　　**10** beats and upbraids his master 主人の義経をたたいてしかる　　**11** by posing as a band of monks collecting funds to restore a temple 寺を修理する資金を集める山伏のふりをして　　**13** tremendous すばらしい **14** besides all the verbal thrust and parry with Togashi 富樫とのせりふのやりとりのほかに　　**18** scroll 巻物 **18** blank 白紙　　**19** extemporizes an appeal for funds in pompous ecclesiastical language 仰々しい仏教の言葉で資金集めの文句を即席にならべる　　**27** struggled to memorize いっしょうけんめいにおぼえようとした　　**31** huddled over ちぢこまった

p. 165 **2** giggled くすくす笑った　　**3** was supposed to remain still じっとしていることになっていた　　**6** ruse 計略　　**9** To have Yoshitsune resisting would ruin the whole plot. 義経がさからったのではぜんぶ台なしだ.　　**11** adamant 頑固 **28** started poking つつきはじめた　　**29** tickling くすぐる **30** armpits わきの下　　**33** was deprived of her role as a monk 山伏の役からおろされた

p. 166 **1** gritted his teeth manfully 男らしく歯をくいしばった **5** left by herself 独りぼっちにされると　　**6** started to improvise a Totto-chan ballet トットちゃん流のバレーをやりはじめた　　**17** amateur drama 学芸会　　**20** had ample opportunity for doing it at school そういうことは学校でたっぷりやれた　　**27** in musical notation 音符にして

p. 167 **1** without encroaching on anyone else's space 人の場所に入らないで

p. 168 **4** at intervals 合間には　　**5** inspect 調べる **10** familiarize themselves with the rhythms リズムをのみ込ませる　　**16** quite a job 大仕事　　**19** spick and span きれいに　　**22** cleaning off graffiti 落書をきれいにする **25** had their fill of scribbling 充分落書を楽しめた **28** manipulate うまく扱う　　**29** connoisseur 目きき

p. 169 **11** were stunned 呆然とした　　**19** crooked まがって **27** with nostalgia なつかしく　　**28** trusted her implicitly 全面的にトットちゃんを信頼した

p. 170 **9** in single file 一列になって　　**13** her first reaction was

227

disbelief トットちゃんは，はじめ信じられなかった

    24 hymn music 賛美歌

p. 171 **2** grubby hand きたない手   **30** made things much harder ますますつらいものにした   **31** conspicuous 目で見えてしまう   **31** saving grace なぐさめ

p. 172 **10** a little more feminine もう少し女性的な   **14** giving injections 注射をうつ   **16** was transported with joy うれしくなった   **26** in his intelligent, resonant voice 頭のよさそうなよく通る声で   **28** to be a spy スパイになるには
    32 bluntly 遠慮なく

p. 173 **4** a chatterbox おしゃべりな子   **5** was dumbfounded びっくりして口もきけなかった   **7** all things she had suspected トットちゃんが不安に思っていたことばかり   **10** out of spite 意地悪で

p. 174 **13** was destined to do something brilliant 何かすてきなことをするにきまっている   **19** mumbled something 何かつぶやいた   **27** make itself felt in the life of Totto-chan and her family トットちゃんや家族の生活の中でも感じられる
    32 comply with 合わせる

p. 175 **2** was making do with で間に合わせていた   **4** was rationed 配給制になった   **7** a vending machine 自動販売機
    10 a very appetizing picture とてもおいしそうな絵
    23 what most would have thought welcome だれでもよろこびそうな   **26** munitions factory 軍需工場   **29** a prestigious musical decoration すばらしい音楽賞

p. 176 **1** scarce 少ない   **2** being called up 招集されている
    12 had barely enough to eat わずかしか食物がなかった
    18 never urged him to do it ぜひやれとは言わなかった
    23 disowned 勘当

p. 177 **4** seemed quite spacious かなり広いように思われた
    11 scrambling onto his back 校長先生の背によじ登る
    11 clamoring for his attention 校長先生の注意をひこうと大声を出して   **13** would remonstrate 抗議するように言ったものだった   **17** the least bit slow ちょっとでもおくれる
    27 after several days' thought 2，3日考えた結果
    28 decided against climbing on his back 校長先生の背によじ登らないことにした   **30** would be more appropriate said face to face 顔を見つめ合って言った方がよいだろう
    31 tilted her head a little 頭をちょっと横に傾むけた

p. 178 **4** expectantly 期待している顔で   **6** in a big-sisterly or motherly way お姉さんかお母さんみたいに   **14** without fail かならず   **26** showing no embarrassment about のことは

まるっきり気にせずに　**30**　made a pledge 誓いをたてた

p. 179 **15**　loaded with bombs 爆弾を積んだ　　**30**　scary ghost stories こわい幽霊のお話

p. 180 **4**　was at the front 戦地にいた　　**18**　the troops in dangerous positions 危険なところにいる軍隊　　**22**　somehow seemed forlorn なんとなくさびしそうに思われた　　**26**　mosquito net かや　　**28**　Long Live the Emperor 天皇陛下万才　　**31**　invariably いつもかならず　　**33**　causing a great fuss 大さわぎになる

p. 181 **6**　was nowhere to be found どこにもいなかった　　**9**　orchid らん　　**13**　there was no sign of の影も形もなかった　　**28**　seemed at a loss for words どう言っていいのかわからなかった

p. 182 **7**　a strong conviction 強い確信　　**11**　keeping her eyes lowered 眼を下にむけたまま

p. 183 **5**　Never tease animals. 決して動物をいじめてはいけない.　　**9**　develop a bad nature たちが悪くなる　　**27**　was finally called up とうとう軍隊に召集された　　**29**　guardian angel 守護神　　**30**　came to the rescue たすけに来た

p. 184 **3**　without so much as a grumble 不平ひとつ言わずに　　**5**　a rousing, send-off tea-party にぎやかに良ちゃんを送り出す茶話会　　**16**　on purpose わざわざ　　**25**　roasted dried squid 焼いたするめ　　**27**　a great luxury たいへんなぜいたく　　**29**　a ration obtainable only for those leaving for the front 出征する人だけに手に入る配給品

p. 185 **11**　funeral dumplings 葬式まんじゅう　　**18**　gave him quite a start 校長先生をびっくりさせた　　**27**　horticulturist 園芸家　　**29**　nursery garden 苗木園

p. 186 **10**　bandaging ほうたいをする

p. 187 **8**　his departure coincided with... 良ちゃんの出征と同時に…がやってきた　　**15**　the house adjoining the school 学校につづいた家　　**18**　incendiary bombs 焼夷弾　　**22**　was enveloped in flames 炎につつまれた　　**22**　the sound he loved so much of children laughing and children singing 校長先生が愛した子供たちの笑い声や歌声　　**24**　was collapsing with a fearful noise 恐ろしい音をたててくずれ落ちた　　**25**　impossible to quench 消し止めるのは不可能で

p. 188 **1**　dumbfounded 茫然として　　**5**　evacuation train 疎開列車

（神奈川大学助教授　斎藤誠毅）

（普及版）英文版 窓ぎわのトットちゃん

TOTTO-CHAN: The Little Girl at the Window

1996年2月　第1刷発行
2004年12月　第11刷発行

著　者　　黒柳徹子

訳　者　　ドロシー・ブリトン

　絵　　　いわさきちひろ

発行者　　畑野文夫

発行所　　講談社インターナショナル株式会社
　　　　　〒112-8652 東京都文京区音羽1-17-14
　　　　　電話　03-3944-6493（編集部）
　　　　　　　　03-3944-6492（営業部・業務部）
　　　　　ホームページ　www.kodansha-intl.com

印刷・製本所　共同印刷株式会社

© 黒柳徹子 1981
Printed in Japan
ISBN4-7700-2067-8

JAPANESE LANGUAGE GUIDES
Easy-to-use guides to essential language skills

13 SECRETS FOR SPEAKING FLUENT JAPANESE
日本語をペラペラ話すための13の秘訣 *Giles Murray*

The most fun, rewarding, and universal techniques of successful learners of Japanese that any-one can put immediately to use. A unique and exciting alternative, full of lively commentaries, comical illustrations, and brain-teasing puzzles.
Paperback, 184 pages; ISBN 4-7700-2302-2

ALL ABOUT PARTICLES   新装版 助詞で変わるあなたの日本語 *Naoko Chino*
The most common and less common particles brought together and broken down into some 200 usages, with abundant sample sentences.
Paperback, 160 pages; ISBN 4-7700-2781-8

JAPANESE VERBS AT A GLANCE   新装版 日本語の動詞 *Naoko Chino*
Clear and straightforward explanations of Japanese verbs—their functions, forms, roles, and politeness levels.
Paperback, 180 pages; ISBN 4-7700-2765-6

BEYOND POLITE JAPANESE: A Dictionary of Japanese Slang and Colloquialisms
新装版 役に立つ話しことば辞典 *Akihiko Yonekawa*

Expressions that all Japanese, but few foreigners, know and use every day. Sample sentences for every entry.
Paperback, 176 pages; ISBN 4-7700-2773-7

BUILDING WORD POWER IN JAPANESE: Using Kanji Prefixes and Suffixes
新装版 増えて使えるヴォキャブラリー *Timothy J. Vance*

Expand vocabulary and improve reading comprehension by modifying your existing lexicon.
Paperback, 128 pages; ISBN 4-7700-2799-0

HOW TO SOUND INTELLIGENT IN JAPANESE: A Vocabulary Builder
新装版 日本語の知的表現 *Charles De Wolf*

Lists, defines, and gives examples for the vocabulary necessary to engage in intelligent conver-sation in fields such as politics, art, literature, business, and science.
Paperback, 160 pages; ISBN 4-7700-2859-8

MAKING SENSE OF JAPANESE: What the Textbooks Don't Tell You
新装版 日本語の秘訣 *Jay Rubin*

"Brief, wittily written essays that gamely attempt to explain some of the more frustrating hurdles [of Japanese].... They can be read and enjoyed by students at any level." —*Asahi Evening News*
Paperback, 144 pages; ISBN 4-7700-2802-4

LOVE, HATE and Everything in Between: Expressing Emotions in Japanese
新装版 日本語の感情表現集 *Mamiko Murakami*

Includes more than 400 phrases that are useful when talking about personal experience and nuances of feeling.
Paperback, 176 pages; ISBN 4-7700-2803-2

JAPANESE LANGUAGE GUIDES
Easy-to-use guides to essential language skills

THE HANDBOOK OF JAPANESE VERBS

日本語動詞ハンドブック　*Taeko Kamiya*

An indispensable reference and guide to Japanese verbs aimed at beginning and intermediate students. Precisely the book that verb-challenged students have been looking for.

• Verbs are grouped, conjugated, and combined with auxiliaries
• Different forms are used in sentences
• Each form is followed by reinforcing examples and exercises

Paperback, 256 pages; ISBN 4-7700-2683-8

THE HANDBOOK OF JAPANESE ADJECTIVES AND ADVERBS

日本語形容詞・副詞ハンドブック　*Taeko Kamiya*

The ultimate reference manual for those seeking a deeper understanding of Japanese adjectives and adverbs and how they are used in sentences. Ideal, too, for those simply wishing to expand their vocabulary or speak livelier Japanese.

Paperback , 336 pages; ISBN 4-7700-2879-2

A HANDBOOK OF COMMON JAPANESE PHRASES

日本語決まり文句辞典　*Sanseido*

Japanese is rich in common phrases perfect for any number and variety of occasions. This handbook lists some 600 of them and explains when, where, and how to use them, providing alternatives for slightly varied circumstances and revealing their underlying psychology.

Paperback, 320 pages; ISBN 4-7700-2798-2

BASIC CONNECTIONS: Making Your Japanese Flow

新装版 日本語の基礎ルール　*Kakuko Shoji*

Explains how words and phrases dovetail, how clauses pair up with other clauses, how sentences come together to create harmonious paragraphs. The goal is to enable the student to speak both coherently and smoothly.

Paperback, 160 pages; ISBN 4-7700-2860-1

JAPANESE CORE WORDS AND PHRASES: Things You Can't Find in a Dictionary

新装版 辞書では解らない慣用表現　*Kakuko Shoji*

Some Japanese words and phrases, even though they lie at the core of the language, forever elude the student's grasp. This book brings these recalcitrants to bay.

Paperback, 144 pages; ISBN 4-7700-2774-5

READ REAL JAPANESE: All You Need to Enjoy Eight Contemporary Writers

新装版 日本語で読もう　*Janet Ashby*

Original Japanese essays by Yoko Mori, Ryuichi Sakamoto, Machi Tawara, Shoichi Nejime, Momoko Sakura, Seiko Ito, Banana Yoshimoto, and Haruki Murakami. With vocabulary lists giving the English for Japanese words and phrases and also notes on grammar, nuance, and idiomatic usage.

Paperback, 168 pages; ISBN 4-7700-2936-5

BREAKING INTO JAPANESE LITERATURE: Seven Modern Classics in Parallel Text

日本語を読むための七つの物語　*Giles Murray*

Read classics of modern Japanese fiction in the original with the aid of a built-in, customized dictionary, free MP3 sound files of professional Japanese narrators reading the stories, and literal English translations. Features Ryunosuke Akutagawa's "Rashomon" and other stories.

Paperback, 240 pages; ISBN 4-7700-2899-7

HAGAKURE   The Book of the Samurai   *Yamamoto Tsunetomo*

Hagakure ("In the Shadow of Leaves") is a manual for the samurai classes consisting of a series of short anecdotes and reflections that give both insight and instruction in the philosophy and code of behavior that foster the true spirit of Bushido—the Way of the Warrior. As featured in the film *Ghost Dog*.

Hardcover, 192 pages; ISBN 4-7700-2916-0   Paperback, 192 pages; ISBN 4-7700-1106-7

THE UNFETTERED MIND
Writings of the Zen Master to the Sword Master   *Soho Takuan*

The philosophy and competitive strategy presented by the spiritual mentor to Musashi is as useful to today's corporate warriors as it was to 17th-century samurai.

Hardcover, 144 pages; ISBN 4-7700-2947-0   Paperback, 104 pages; ISBN 0-87011-851-X

THE LIFE-GIVING SWORD
Secret Teachings from the House of the Shogun   *Yagyu Munenori*

This is the new and definitive English translation of the classic text on the art of the No-Sword by seventeeth-century swordsman Yagyu Munenori. It is a treasury of proven Zen wisdom that will be of interest to anyone in business or politics, as well as practitioners of the martial arts.

Hardcover: 192 pages; ISBN 4-7700-2955-5

BUSHIDO   The Soul of Japan   *Inazo Nitobe*

Written specifically for a Western audience in 1900 by Japan's under-secretary general to the League of Nations, *Bushido* explains concepts such as honor and loyalty within traditional Japanese ethics. The book is a classic, and as such throws a great deal of light on Japanese thinking and behavior, both past and present.

Hardcover , 160 pages; ISBN 4-7700-2731-1

THE BOOK OF FIVE RINGS   *Miyamoto Musashi*

Setting down his thoughts on swordplay, on winning, and on spirituality, legendary swordsman Miyamoto Musashi intended this modest work as a guide for his immediate disciples and future generations of samurai. He had little idea he was penning a masterpiece that would be eagerly devoured by people in all walks of life centuries after his death.

Hardcover, 160 pages; ISBN 4-7700-2801-6

MUSASHI   An Epic Novel of the Samurai Era   *Eiji Yoshikawa*

This classic work tells of the legendary samurai who was the greatest swordsman of all time. ". . . a stirring saga . . . one that will prove popular not only for readers interested in Japan but also for those who simply want a rousing read."—*The Washington Post*

Hardcover, 984 pages; ISBN 4-7700-1957-2

THE LONE SAMURAI
The Life of Miyamoto Musashi   *William Scott Wilson*

The Lone Samurai is a landmark biography of Miyamoto Musashi, the legendary Japanese figure known throughout the world as a master swordsman, spiritual seeker, and author of *The Book of Five Rings*. Includes photographs, maps, glossary, and appendices.

Hardcover: 288 pages: ISBN 4-7700-2942-X